HOW TO INCREASE SALES
and PUT YOURSELF
ACROSS BY TELEPHONE

HOW
TO INCREASE
SALES

PRENTICE-HALL, INC. — ENGLEWOOD CLIFFS, N. J.

and PUT YOURSELF ACROSS BY TELEPHONE

by Mona Ling

How to Increase Sales and Put Yourself Across by Telephone
by Mona Ling
Published by Prentice-Hall, Inc., Englewood Cliffs, N.J.

0–13–413138–X

Printed in the United States of America

Prentice–Hall International, Inc., London
Prentice–Hall of Australia, Pty. Ltd., Sydney
Prentice–Hall of Canada, Ltd., Toronto
Prentice–Hall of India Private Ltd., New Delhi
Prentice–Hall of Japan, Inc., Tokyo

20 19 18 17 16 15 14 13 12

CONTENTS

PART III   MODERN USE OF THE TELEPHONE

USING
the
TELEPHONE
to
SELL

∿∿∿∿∿∿∿∿∿∿∿∿∿∿∿∿∿∿∿∿∿∿∿∿∿∿ PART **I**

THE CREATION
OF A VERBAL UNIVERSE

Don't keep forever on the public roads. Leave the beaten track occasionally and dive into the woods. You will be certain to find something that you have never seen before. One discovery will lead to another, and before you know it you will have something worth thinking about to occupy your mind.

ALEXANDER GRAHAM BELL

WHEN Alexander Graham Bell said, "Don't keep forever on the public roads," he was speaking about the discovery of new ideas and inventions. He was not speaking about the "people who would leave the public roads" because of a shortage of gasoline.

When Mr. Bell invented the telephone, he did not know how valuable the instrument would become in our society. The people in our society did not know how valuable the telephone would become until there was a shortage of fuel and limited travel.

THE ENERGY CRISIS

As 1973 was coming to an end, the Mideast masters of the world's most productive oil fields took action which altered the international energy equation for years to come. Their action forced Americans out of their cars within a few days after the news reached the motorists. The expressways were no longer crammed curb to curb with underpopulated automobiles. The long lines were at the gasoline stations trying to buy gas at any price. **3**

In two surprise strokes, the mideast oil barons dramatically changed the life-style of Americans. They raised the price of crude oil which ended the long era of cheap energy and cancelled shipments of oil to the United States. Within a few weeks gasoline stations were closed on Sundays and short of gasoline on weekdays.

The Administration is depending on public cooperation with voluntary conservation measures. In early January, year-round daylight saving time took effect, which experts estimate could conserve thousands of barrels of oil daily. However, other fuel-saving measures are being proposed, such as closing gas stations another day in addition to Sunday and proposing a partial ban on driving one day a week.

The government has released details of its contingency gasoline-rationing system. If and when it goes into effect, the program might limit licensed drivers to between 32 and 35 gallons of gasoline per month. Special arrangements are to be made for taxi drivers, doctors, others who need more gas than ordinary motorists.

HANG-UPS AHEAD

Officials believe that the United States faces years of adjusting to fuel scarcity. For the longer range, the energy outlook is potentially very bright. Most officials believe that the next five years will be extremely difficult for the motorist.

The consumer, businessman, executive, and salesman will be affected somewhat by limited travel. Many people depend on their automobiles for social and business contacts. The scarcity of fuel will take people out of their automobiles and put them into their homes and offices. Their communications will be by telephone. The majority of people can easily take care of personal matters and business matters by telephone with a reduction of time and cost. The greatest hardship will be for the salesman who spends most of the time in his automobile to conduct his business. The salesman's automobile is an "extension of his legs." The salesman who depends on his automobile for business will have to make drastic changes in his work. The telephone will be used to initiate business, make appointments for sales interviews, and to keep in touch. The telephone to some extent will become a substitute for many face-to-face calls.

TELEPHONES FOR BUSINESS

Fortunately, the majority of businessmen and executives can conduct their business by telephone. At the present time the businessman and executive use the voice telephone for most of their communications. However, the picture phone or video phone is beginning to emerge. The executive can look forward to speaking with his clients and associates face-to-face as well as voice-to-voice.

The video and high-speed data service is prompting increasing speculation about new communication facilities. Tomorrow's businessman is promised the ability to talk face-to-face with associates and clients regardless of distance. He can participate in nationwide and worldwide meetings without leaving his office. He can perform a large number of executive functions from his office which would result in reduced executive travel and expense. It would increase the time available for other activities. The relatively high cost would limit the use of the videotelephone to top executives or key employees.

TELEPHONES FOR SALESMEN

The voice telephone will continue to be the major telecommunications terminal for the salesman. It is universally available. People have learned to use it as a way of life. It is inexpensive, saves time and energy. Each telephone in the country has a number. To get the one you want takes only a few seconds.

When man began the long process of building up complex environments, societies, nations and established a verbal universe, he required faster communication. Through the centuries man has progressed from one medium to another to widen the range and scope of communication with others, until today the telephone links the world and provides man and nations with vast communication facilities. The telephone may become the most important invention in our century.

WHY TELEPHONE SKILLS
WILL INCREASE SALES

*It is more than probable that the average man could, with no
injury to his health, increase his efficiency fifty per cent.*

WALTER DILL SCOTT

TO MY KNOWLEDGE no statistical surveys have been
made that would indicate the different types of prospecting activities in which various firms are engaged. However, broad observation has indicated that most salesmen make selling through personal visits their primary objective. This observation has been
made from business, manufacturing, and trading enterprises that
employed a half dozen salesmen to those that employed thousands.

PERSONAL VISITS

Most salesmen visit prospective buyers at their places of business. These trips consume a great part of the salesman's working
day. Because of time-consuming travel and other nonselling duties,
very little of the day is actually spent in prospecting and selling.
The largest selling expense is that of *personal* selling.

Unfortunately, most of the data on wasted time, sales, or profits,
as a result of ineffective prospecting, is dumped into other expenses. If the expense of inefficient prospecting methods, ineffective telephone calls, wasted time and visits could be accurately determined, exclusive of all other expenses, sales managers and
salesmen would be convinced of the value of developing telephone

6

skills. For the telephone is the point at which the salesman with a professional technique succeeds in saving *time* and *money*. Using the telephone to obtain a sales interview is essential for the purpose of saving time, energy, and travel expense. Upon occasion, it may prevent a trip to see a "suspect" instead of a prospect.

Al N. Sears, vice-president of Remington Rand, Inc., said, "Of all the various methods for the solicitation of sales—personal calls by salesmen, advertising, sales promotion, catalogs, expositions, direct mail, personal letters—salesmen's calls are by far the most costly. Authentic surveys and authoritative sources indicate that outside salesmen spent 50 per cent of their time with customers and prospects; 38 per cent traveling and waiting for interviews; 12 per cent on reports, office work, and other details.

"Out of the total of 1,952 working hours available in the 244 working days of a year, a salesman devotes just 976 hours to presenting his product story." [1]

THE TELEPHONE INCREASES SALES

When my headquarters were in Los Angeles, I received a telephone call from an insurance agent who wanted to see if I could be of assistance to him in his prospecting problems. Peter Hyun owned a casualty insurance business and was an agent for American National Insurance Company. He was interested in increasing his sales in life insurance. Here are a few of Peter's problems that he wanted to solve:

1. *Wasted time.* Peter was spending most of his time driving around the Los Angeles area in an attempt to catch prospects in their offices or homes. He was spending more time in his car than he was spending anywhere else, and wasn't seeing enough prospects to compensate him for his time and efforts.

2. *Wasted expense.* Driving a car around the vast Los Angeles area every day was expensive, as was parking. Peter's sales did not compensate him for the expense that was incurred in travel.

---

[1] Charles B. Roth, *Successful Sales Presentations* (Englewood Cliffs, N. J.: Prentice-Hall), p. VII.

3. *Wasted energy.* He was working long hours without obtaining enough results to show for his efforts. He was in constant motion, or so it seemed, without accomplishing anything.

4. *Not enough prospects.* Peter did not see enough prospects in proportion to the long hours he worked and the amount of time he invested in traveling around the city.

5. *Not enough sales.* Though Peter's closing ratio of sales was high, he was not closing enough sales to meet his anticipated goals. The primary reason was that he was not having enough selling interviews to close the sales he needed to reach his goals.

6. *Low goals.* Peter had many fine abilities but had become discouraged because of poor results in prospecting. He had lowered his goals to an unrealistic figure.

7. *Ineffective work pattern.* Peter's habit of driving around the city to locate prospects without firm appointments was time-consuming. He could not follow a define work pattern. He worked on a hit-or-miss basis. If he found a prospect in, he gave a sales presentation; if he did not find a prospect in, he would go to another prospect's home or office or return to his office.

8. *Incomplete records.* Peter did not keep score of his personal visits, the number of contacts, the hours spent in travel and waiting. He did not keep up-to-date records on his sales performance; therefore he could not determine his weak points or take steps to correct them.

As Peter had a casualty business that took considerable time to manage, we worked out a schedule that would enable him to devote the major part of time from Monday through Wednesday on life-insurance selling. He was expected to call a predetermined number of prospects in one area and arrange interviews with them. We established production goals, arranged time for office duties and telephone practice, and arranged an effective work pattern.

In sessions with insurance agents, it was customary for me to establish a minimum production figure of $25,000 for their first week. Peter felt this figure was high but agreed to follow my suggestions on telephone technique, time-control, and prospecting procedures. I assured him that he could close $25,000 in business within seventy-two hours if he followed the suggestions that had been given in this session, which, incidentally, was our first training session.

Within seventy-two hours, Peter had sold $130,000 in life insurance, which was more than he had sold during the past three months. Within thirty days he had sold more life insurance than he had sold during any year of his career. I might add that Peter sold this amount during the month of July, with the loss of the Fourth of July holiday. Also, the month of July is not considered to be one of the best sales months in California.

Peter had many fine abilities. He was sincere, honest, gave excellent service and was extremely conscientious in every phase of his work. After working out an organized pattern, he was able to shorten his day by approximately two hours. He was delighted, as this gave him more time to spend with his wife and children. He was more efficient in his work because he had more time to concentrate on the many phases of his business. Peter was able to arrange most of his weekly appointments within approximately one hour, with perhaps a few additional calls to prospects who could not be reached during normal working hours. With definite appointments, he was able to eliminate wasted time, money, and energy.

"Nothing in my career has been more helpful to my advancement, growth, and personal development than the knowledge I gained from telephone technique. I think telephone technique can mean the difference between mediocrity and success for a salesman." Peter added, "Poor telephone technique seems to be a common denominator of the majority of salesmen. Telephone technique is vital to any man who wishes to rise above the majority."

Peter had been reluctant to use the telephone prior to his training in telephone technique because he had a fear that the prospect would say "no." He now qualified his prospects on the telephone and welcomed a definite "no" or indication of lack of interest. He soon discovered that he could eliminate suspects and spend his time talking to prospects.

When a salesman learns a technique of prospecting by telephone, he can increase the number of prospects and sales within hours. He can figuratively establish a bank account into which he can deposit as much money as he wishes. He can also control scientifically his production and his earnings.

The major failure of most salesmen can be traced to an ineffective prospecting system. Many salesmen are using horse-and-buggy methods of prospecting to tell the story of twentieth century improvements and progress. The most effective and practical method of prospecting today is through the use of the telephone.

For a salesman, the shortest distance between two points is not a straight line but a telephone line. However, the salesman who has a telephone and doesn't know how to use it is no better off than the salesman who doesn't have one.

RELUCTANCE TO USE THE TELEPHONE

Many firms that have been in business for a long period of time have built up certain traditional prospecting methods. They have not explored the possibilities of new methods. Many executives of these firms believe that telephone solicitation is not suited to their particular product or market. For the most part, the suggestion to use the telephone in the solicitation of appointments had been discarded without any attempt to study the impact this sales tool might have in increased sales and profits. The executives who have made a study of the telephone as a sales tool and who have incorporated it into their prospecting system have increased appointments, sales, and profits.

Many of the firms that are reluctant to incorporate the telephone into their sales program may be basing their attitudes on the fact that some companies are criticized because of their telephone system. It is true that many companies have damaged their reputations by permitting untrained, unprofessional persons to telephone, soliciting business or making appointments. When a company is unwilling to train its telephone sales personnel or salesmen to work as efficiently at the telephone as they do at other tasks, it may expect to receive criticism from the customers, potential buyers, and the public.

To insure the same standards of excellence of performance in the use of the telephone as are obtained in other duties, a telephone training program should be incorporated into the company sales program. A representative of a firm who has been thoroughly trained in a professional telephone technique will not damage the reputation of the firm. The untrained representative will damage the reputation of that firm.

PROSPECTING PROBLEM-SOLVING

The sales manager of a large firm told me that they had been reluctant to use the telephone as a prospecting tool because other firms had abused the telephone, had violated good taste in the use of it, and had created an unfavorable image on the mind of the public.

"We have a good reputation and want to keep it," he said bluntly. "But the only way we know to increase sales is to increase the number of interviews for each salesman, and the only way to do that is to make definite appointments.

"Los Angeles is a large area, and my men lose time in driving around the city, trying to find a place to park, and waiting for the prospective buyer to get to the office or to get time to see them.

"My men can close a sale if they can get into the office of the prospect." He added, "Their difficulty is in getting prospects."

He paused for a moment, then said, "I don't mind telling you that we aren't too enthusiastic about the idea of using the telephone. We have been trying to use the telephone for several days and we've all been flops."

That was understandable, as salesmen who have not been properly trained in telephone technique and communication skills would not be expected to perform as skillfully as those who had received training. If the salesman has difficulty in expressing himself in a personal interview, he might carry a sign that says, "I really have great ideas but am unable to express them." Or he can show testimonials, samples, displays, or even films to dramatize his sales presentation. At the point of the telephone, the salesman needs technique to express his ideas and persuade the prospective buyer to grant an interview. His technique must be expressed through tone, emotional color, speech, and words that create a mental image in the mind of the prospect. Do-it-yourself efforts, however honest and sincere, usually fail to produce the desired results.

THE TELEPHONE SAVES TIME

The sales manager made arrangements for a telephone program for his salesmen to explore the possibilities of the use of the telephone in obtaining appointments. Our first session revealed many weaknesses in the current prospecting program. Here are a few of the questions that were asked to pinpoint weaknesses.

How do you spend your time each day?
Time spent in sales interviews   _____
Time spent in travel and waiting   _____
Time spent in office work and other details   _____

The purpose of an analysis of the salesman's time spent in sales interviews, travel and waiting, and office work is to determine his weak points in time-control. The result is that appraisal of each salesman's time-control figures will reveal weak points, and quick action can be taken in correcting them. To a salesman, *time is money.* If the salesman is losing *time,* he is losing *money.*

In our over-all picture, the average salesman spent approximately 40 per cent of his time in sales interviews, 45 per cent of his time in travel and waiting, and 15 per cent of his time in office work and other details.

Our immediate goal was to reduce wasted time spent in travel and waiting and to increase the time spent in sales interviews.

How much time does it take to reach your prospect's office?
The answers for individual salesmen varied from "fifteen minutes" to "two hours." Every salesman admitted that he spent a great deal of time in driving to see his prospects and in trying to find a parking place. We checked the times given against the time that it takes to reach a prospect on the telephone.

You can dial a telephone number in *ten seconds*. You can reach your prospect within *ten to thirty seconds,* calling from the comfort of your air-conditioned office. There are no traffic or parking problems, and no waiting time spent in an outer office. Your call goes directly to the prospect in most cases.

How much time does it take to get inside your prospect's office to give your sales presentation?

The answers of individual salesmen ranged from fifteen minutes to an hour or more. Some salesmen admitted that, after waiting for a long period of time, they had not been able to get into some of their prospective buyer's offices at all. We checked the times given against the time that it takes to reach a prospect on the telephone and arrange a firm appointment.

Here is the time you can expect to arrange a firm appointment, if you know an effective telephone technique. You can dial in *ten seconds*, will probably wait *twenty seconds* for the answer, and will obtain the appointment in most cases within *180 seconds*. To arrange a firm interview with a prospect under favorable conditions, you can expect to spend approximately *210 seconds*.

When you speak directly to the prospect, you have the opportunity of making a good impression and of getting him sufficiently interested in your idea, so that you will be received under favorable circumstances. For the most part, your chances of speaking directly to the prospect are greater on the telephone than they are in person. Many prospects, potential buyers, businessmen, or executives answer their own telephones. The potential buyer will grant telephone time more readily than office time.

Here are some of the responses these particular salesmen were receiving on cold personal visits:

1. Mr. Smith is in a conference.
2. Mr. Smith is on the telephone.
3. Mr. Smith is leaving the city today.
4. Mr. Smith is not in. We don't know when to expect him.
5. Mr. Smith is in. Do you have an appointment?
6. Mr. Smith is out of the city.
7. Mr. Smith is in but is busy. Could you come back?

A brief telephone call will save a trip and will indicate the availability of the prospect for an interview.

The salesmen soon learned the great saving of their valuable time in spending *180 seconds* to *210 seconds* to discover whether their prospect was in, or busy, or out of the city, or available for an interview.

CALLS DETERMINE SALES

Basic to the successful operation of any business is the activity of prospecting. Every sales manager and salesman knows that sales will increase with effective telephone calls to make appointments, and with increased personal calls. Other things being equal, the greater the number of calls, the greater the number of sales; the greater the number of sales, the greater the profits of the firm. Telephone calls that will accomplish good results with a minimum expenditure of time, money, and energy are necessary for the vast majority of salesmen in business, manufacturing, and trading enterprises. The most modern and aggressive firms build a sales program that includes telephone techniques that utilize the telephone to its greatest advantage.

How many telephone calls do you have to make to obtain the sales interviews necessary to meet your goals?

You can dial twenty-five numbers in one hour and talk to fifteen or sixteen persons. An inexperienced salesman might obtain two or three appointments out of the exposure of talking to fifteen persons. However, experienced salesmen obtain one appointment out of every two or three conversations. Many salesmen maintain an average of one appointment out of every three calls; some salesmen average three appointments out of every four calls, particularly if they are calling referrals.

Keep a record of the calls you make each hour, the number of persons you ask for appointments, and the number of appointments you obtain. In this way you can improve your technique and your ratio. Your ratio should be used as a measure of your effort, knowledge, and performance. Your ratio also reflects your knowledge of human nature, sales techniques, speech, listening, as well as your ability to overcome objections and to close appointments. Only by self-analysis, with constructive ideas as to how to correct errors or weaknesses, can you hope to become efficient in the use of the telephone.

Through the effective use of the telephone, these salesmen were able to increase their interviews to four each day, with a total of twenty each week for each salesman. Their ratios of appointments had been "rough" the first week but gradually improved to one appointment out of every three cold calls and nine appointments out of every ten referral calls. The entire group of salesmen decreased driving time from 45 per cent to 25 per cent and increased sales from 40 per cent to 60 per cent.

You might check these figures against your time spent in travel and waiting, and your time spent in actual selling interviews.

CONSISTENCY IS IMPORTANT

By focusing to the telephone all activities of prospecting, arranging appointments, confirming appointments, and some service calls, these salesmen discovered that they could work on a more efficient basis. They discovered, too, they could be more consistent in prospecting and in keeping in touch with customers and potential buyers.

Here are some of the suggestions these salesmen followed in their daily prospecting schedule:

1. Set a definite number of calls to make each day.
2. Set a definite time to call each day.
3. Check on the best time to call occupations, businessmen, professional persons, and customers.
4. Expect to arrange a definite number of interviews during each telephoning session.
5. Complete all calls that are on your list during each telephoning session.
6. Keep a score of appointments to calls during each session.

7. When you obtain an interview, dial another number quickly. Don't stop for a cup of coffee. You are closer to another appointment immediately after having obtained an appointment than at any other time.

8. Don't make an analysis of your calls during the session. Make your analysis of calls after the session.

9. Schedule appointments for every Monday during the following weeks. Always be employed on Monday of each week.

10. Don't be unemployed during productive time. During unproductive sales hours, schedule appointments in advance for productive times.

MAKE PROSPECTING SECOND NATURE

"Prospecting should be made a regular part of any salesman's activity," says Charles L. Lapp, Ph.D., professor of marketing at Washington University, St. Louis, Missouri. "If you will look around in your industry, you will find that most of the year-in and year-out high volume sales producers are good prospectors and are continually prospecting."

Chuck Lapp trains over 100,000 salesmen each year throughout the United States and in other countries. He is the author of several books on prospecting and sales techniques. Two of his books are *Training and Supervising Salesmen* and *Personal Supervision of Salesmen* (Business Book Company, St. Louis, Mo.). In these books Chuck expresses this idea: "If you don't do a little prospecting all the time, you will soon find yourself going out of business as a salesman."

The call that one salesman makes in one company may differ substantially from the call made by another salesman in another company. Yet each salesman is concerned primarily with locating prospective buyers for his product or service.

It has been my observation in the training of many salesmen and saleswomen that they are inclined to follow a consistent pattern of prospecting, if they know a telephone technique. After being shown techniques that others have found successful, each salesman will naturally select and perfect a system of prospecting which will enable him to obtain more satisfactory results with a minimum of time, expense, and effort. After using a consistent system of prospecting for a period of time, prospecting does become second nature to the salesman.

INCREASED SALES FIVE TIMES

Howard Richard, C.L.U., with New York Life in Boston, says "The biggest difference between mediocrity and success is the salesman's skill in using the telephone for prospecting and closing sales."

From the day he joined his company in 1935 until he entered the United States Army in 1942, Howard Richard was moderately successful. Being in the service gave him a chance to make an objective analysis of his prospecting methods. He decided that he had wasted time and energy in going from place to place, waiting to see prospective clients. He had also wasted time seeing unproductive people. He estimated that he could reach ten times as many persons in a day through the effective use of the telephone.

When Howard returned to the life insurance business from service, he discovered that selling over the telephone was twice as difficult as selling in person, but he could reach *ten times* as many persons in a day. The result was *five times as many sales*. His first year back from service saw Howard reaching the million-dollar sales mark. His sales have continued to soar. For the past several years, he has been his company's top producer in individual sales for New England and New York. He sells a policy a day from $10,000 to $30,000, with an average total of three hundred individual sales each year. His total sales each year are over $5,000,000, exclusive of group insurance and pension plans.

MAKE SALES CLIMB INSTEAD OF SLUMP DURING A CONVENTION WITH A LEARN-BY-DOING TELEPHONE SELLING SESSION

Leonard Pfaelzer, of Pfaelzer Brothers, Chicago, has given me permission to use one of his actual learn-by-doing telephone selling sessions that was used by his company during a sales conference, and that was reported by The Dartnell Corporation in one of its sales training bulletins entitled: *Using the Telephone to Sell.*[2]

When a company pulls its entire sales force into headquarters for a meeting, sales volume usually reflects the absence of personal contact. Not so when Pfaelzer Brothers, Inc. decides to bring its men together. It recently held a five-day sales meeting in Chicago and booked orders exceeding normal weekly sales volume without one salesman seeing a prospect or customer face-to-face.

"More Effective Telephone Selling" was the answer to the problem, as well as the title of a learn-by-doing workshop session that provided a highlight of the meeting. With a strong assist from the Telephone Company, Pfaelzer's sales management group provided each salesman with an organized approach to getting more orders over the telephone. This was presented to the group, with the aid of many well-designed visuals, by Special Accounts Manager Jack Colovitch.

Then to get these principles into action, groups of four or five salesmen, seated together at round tables, discussed ways and means of applying the ideas to specific products and customers. Each man developed his own special telephone sales talk and tried it out on the others in the group. Group members then made suggestions for improvement, added new ideas from their own experiences, and pointed out faults, if any.

Thus, in a short period of time, each man, with the help of his colleagues, was able to conduct several experiments, get reactions to them, and listen to the ideas of others for good things that could be adapted to his own use.

Then came the action. A "Telephone Sales Center" had been set up in an adjacent room. Fifteen individual telephones were ready for calls. The Telephone Company provided these special facilities and assigned an individual "sequence operator" to each telephone. These operators had been provided with lists of customers marked in the order that was best for calls to be placed. In this manner, while a salesman was talking to one customer, the

---

2 *Using the Telephone to Sell* is reprinted through the courtesy of The Dartnell Corporation, Chicago, Ill.

operator was making connections with the next name on the list and always had one party ready to talk as soon as a salesman completed the previous call.

This method of sequence calling made it possible for each salesman to talk to as many as fifteen customers in the hour set aside each day for this personal contact with accounts.

Pfaelzer Brothers, Inc. operates nationally, selling high quality meat, fish, poultry, and other food products to outstanding restaurants, hotels, clubs, hospitals, and other institutions. They are proud of being known as "The House of Personalized Service"— a reputation that has been built up by many years of knowledge and experience in this highly competitive field. An important part of this kind of selling depends on frequent and intelligent personal contact with buyers on the part of each salesman. It is partly because of this background of personal calls during the other fifty-one weeks of the year that most salesmen were able to equal or exceed their best previous sales records by means of telephone calls during the week of the convention. The other big reason for the success of this "Telephone Blitz" was the intensive use of a well-planned telephone selling technique—a skill that each man will now carry with him for further use in making telephone contacts during the balance of the year.

As Leonard Pfaelzer, president of the company, puts it: "The knowledge and enthusiasm gained by the men during the meetings were channeled immediately and effectively via the telephone, and we feel that other companies could well profit by our experience. We believe this special session was responsible for our not only maintaining our normal weekly sales volume but exceeding it."

Our thanks to Mr. Pfaelzer, to his national sales manager, Elexis McGrath, and to Ralph Ackley, of Illinois Bell Telephone Company, for their cooperation in sharing this material.

CUSTOMER SERVICE INCREASES SALES

In the April 1962 issue of *The American Salesman*, a time-saving item appeared. "Don't dial M for money, dial 559-5471," urges New York's First National City Bank, which has started all-day, all-night loan service by telephone. Customers can call in information, pick up check next business morning, avoid week-end shopping delays.

Customer telephone shopping can be profitable for stores with improved telephone shopping operations. There are many million working wives, aside from single women, who have little time for shopping except during lunch hours or on an occasional Saturday. Many million housewives have small children to care for, and sitters are scarce during store hours. Being able to dispose of many of their shopping problems quickly and conveniently by telephone naturally appeals to these women. All they need is to be reminded often enough that the service is available through your store.

Today's woman is more involved with neighborhood activities, her family, working, watching television. With less time for shopping, today's woman is—or can be—an enthusiastic *telephone customer*. A quick call to your store easily fits into her stepped-up daily program of daily activities.

A. H. Burchfield, president of Joseph Horne Company, Pittsburgh, says, "In the operation of the Joseph Horne Company, communications play an important role. We rely on the telephone for a large percentage of our incoming customer orders. Telephone Company representatives are capable and willing at all times to suggest and provide the services essential to our growing business."

Telephone shopping can often be made efficient and productive with minimum capital outlays. In many cases stores have vastly improved their operations, merely by sharpening up their *existing* facilities. The stores that have sharpened their facilities have reported substantial increases in sales.

DIALS PROFIT WITH PHONE SALES SYSTEM

In the February 1962 issue of *Sales Management*,[3] a problem and a solution were given. The problem: To find an effective way

---

[3] "Dials Profit with Phone Sales System" is reprinted through the courtesy of *Sales Management*.

to establish a large number of new dealerships quickly—and to serve them at a minimum cost.

The solution: A hand-tailored telephone sales system.

When leadership of the company changed hands in 1957, a 3-man management team at Muntz TV faced a large-screen problem: sales were a piddling $4.5 million a year; losses were running over $1 million. What to do for a company that had been one of the pioneers among television set manufacturers?

During its TV heydays, the Muntz organization spent $13 million promoting the Muntz TV set. But by 1957 the company was so deep in the red that bankruptcy looked like a better-than-even possibility. Then, instead of bowing to what seemed the inevitable, the firm reorganized from top to bottom.

New management has followed a different, sounder, more conservative course. And with a unique telephone sales system, the company has come back into the black. Sales for the fiscal year ending August 31, 1961, were $9.1 million and profits were $832,000.

But in that bleak year 1957 only fifty dealers in the entire United States were handling Muntz TV sets. The new president, Wallace A. Keil, and his team (Jack Simberg, vice-president-sales, and Daniel A. Domin, secretary-treasurer) worked up an unorthodox but effective method of selling and marketing that flew in the face of accepted industry practice.

Gone would be the business of owning factory outlets, as Muntz had. Instead, Muntz would go direct to independent retailers. And to reach these dealers the *telephone sales system* was born. For three years now, the telephone has been the only outside salesman at Muntz TV.

The staff consists of six girls and three men, who utilize long-distance calls and personalized selling techniques to establish dealerships throughout the nation. Other TV set manufacturers openly scoffed. But Muntz is having a quiet last laugh. Results prove its system works. In three years, the company's dealer roster has jumped from fifty to two thousand. Sales, the top brass believe, will hit $12 million next year.

Muntz works up prospect lists for a target area through several methods. First, contacts are via a direct-mail brochure. Potential dealerships in large cities are turned over to a 3-man staff that follows up with personal telephone contacts. These men devote their time to servicing and selling the company's major accounts. Prospects in smaller cities and towns are contacted by six persuasive saleswomen, also by telephone. Simberg personally handles the largest customers and all private-label business.

The women handle ten-state areas, service an average of 250 accounts. Each account gets a call about once a fortnight. In addition, the women make contact with ten to fifteen new accounts every day. The staff is trained to keep conversations friendly and, if possible, on a first-name basis. Already Muntz has about 1.5 per cent of the national retail television market. "Give us three years," says the management, "and we'll have 3 per cent."

Arthur H. ("Red") Motley, one of America's twelve master salesmen and president and publisher of *Parade*, said, "There is nothing wrong with the basic economy that can't be helped with a better job of selling."

Most sales managers and salesmen will agree with that statement. Most sales managers and salesmen will also agree that "There is nothing wrong with selling that can't be helped with a better job of prospecting."

TELE-TECK PROSPECTING QUIZ

Ask yourself the following questions to determine your strong and weak points of prospecting. There are certain prospecting habits without which you can scarcely expect to succeed in competition with others. Question yourself in regard to each point. Assign a value of ten points to each *yes* answer. Those questions that you answer *no* will show your weak spots.

	YES	NO
1. Do you set your production goals in advance?	____	____
2. Do you set high goals?	____	____
3. Do you follow a certain pattern to reach your goals?	____	____
4. Do you prospect systematically?	____	____
5. Do you set definite times to call prospects?	____	____
6. Do you call a predetermined number of prospects?	____	____
7. Do you keep score of appointments to calls?	____	____
8. Do you schedule appointments in advance?	____	____
9. Do you make the most of your prospecting time?	____	____
10. Is the greater part of your day spent in sales activities?	____	____

HOW TO PREPARE
AND ORGANIZE
FOR TELEPHONING

The most valuable result of all education is the ability to make yourself do the thing you have to do when it ought to be done, whether you want to do it or not.

ALDOUS HUXLEY

PROSPECTING is a system of finding potenital buyers on a preselected basis. The history of salesmanship is, to some extent, a record of prospecting. A salesman should have definite objectives and goals to give his work direction and power. A salesman should have an organized systematic plan that will enable him to meet his objectives and attain his goals.

As an organized prospecting system will enable a salesman to attain his goals, the level upon which it is conducted is a matter of great importance. The study of a telephone technique finds its highest justification in the fact that it provides a salesman with skills that enable him to prospect in an organized manner, reaching his goals with a minimum of time and effort. An organized method of prospecting, combined with the knowledge of a telephone technique, will enable a salesman to increase his production and earnings, conserve energy, and save wasted time.

There is a great deal of misunderstanding as to the purpose of keeping records on prospecting activities and results obtained. Records merely indicate weak points that may be corrected quickly without loss of production or earnings.

FOUR BASIC TASKS OF SALESMEN

The salesman has four basic tasks:

1. To find prospective buyers with whom he can arrange personal interviews under favorable circumstances.
2. To inform the prospective buyers of the product or service so as to influence his attitude in a way favorable to the product or service.
3. To persuade the prospective buyer to purchase the product or service, immediately or subsequently.
4. To render quality service so the buyer will continue to do business with that salesman and his firm.

One of the first questions that a salesman new to the business asks: "Where are my prospects?" Prospecting is a problem to some salesmen throughout their entire careers. Other problems arise and are solved, but the problem of prospecting goes on forever—unless, of course, the salesman learns how to prospect in an organized way and develops an effective method.

SOURCES OF PROSPECTS

Your firm should be able to give you your best sources, markets, potential buyers, and to show you how to reach them. For the salesman who does not have a formal training program, these suggestions on general lists might be helpful.

Acquaintances	Lodge
Chamber of Commerce lists	Neighbors
Church groups	Property owners lists
Civic enterprises	Relatives
Clients	Sales lists
Club members	School alumni
Directories	Telephone directories
Executive business lists	Trade and legal journals
Friends	Zone centers of influence

BEST TIME TO CALL

Because timing of the call is extremely important, here is a schedule of the best times to call the various professions and occupations.[1] These suggestions as to the best time to call might vary somewhat in some cities or communities. Make notes beside the various professions and occupations to indicate your best local time to call.

Attorneys	between 3:00 and 5:00 P.M.
Chemists	between 4:00 and 5:00 P.M.
Clergymen	between Monday and Friday
Contractors	before 9:00 A.M.—after 5:00 P.M.
Dentists	before 9:30 A.M.
Druggists	between 1:00 and 3:00 P.M.
Engineers	between 2:00 and 4:00 P.M.
Executives	after 10:30 A.M.
Farmers	between 3:00 and 5:00 P.M.
Government employees	at home—7:00 to 9:00 P.M.
Government officials	between 2:00 and 5:00 P.M.
Grocers	between 1:00 and 3:00 P.M.
Housewives	between 10:00 and 11:00 A.M.
	between 2:00 and 4:00 P.M.
Low-salaried people	call at home
Merchants	after 10:30 A.M.
Morticians	between 10:00 and 11:00 A.M.
Newspapermen	between 2:00 and 5:00 P.M.
Nurses	between 7:00 and 9:00 P.M.
Physicians	between 9:00 and 11:00 A.M.
	between 1:00 and 3:00 P.M.
Printers	between 3:00 and 5:00 P.M.
Public accountants	avoid Jan. 15 through April 15.
Publishers	after 3:00 P.M.
Salesmen	between 9:00 and 11:00 A.M.
Schoolteachers	at home between 7:00 and 9:00 A.M.
Secretaries	between 10:00 and 11:00 A.M. and 2:00 and 4:00 P.M.
Stock brokers	before 10:00 A.M.—after 3:00 P.M.

PROSPECTING METHODS

There are many ways to prospect for business through the use of the telephone: cold calls, prestige referrals, direct mail, personalized letters, and service calls.

---

[1] "Best Time to Call Schedule" is reprinted through the courtesy of Success Motivation Institute, Inc., Waco, Texas, from the recording *How to Get Appointments by Telephone* by Mona Ling.

Cold calls

Many salesmen who are inexperienced learn to prospect by calling from various directories, lists, journals, newspapers, and other sources. These men expose themselves to many people during the first few months of their career.

They learn how to talk to people, evoke the proper responses, handle different personalities, overcome objections, and close quickly. Some salesmen who acquire skills in telephoning become very successful at making cold calls and never learn to prospect any other way.

Here are some suggestions for the organization of your work in making cold calls:

1. Have lists and telephone numbers ready before calling.
2. Have a supply of 3 x 5 cards on your desk for recording names and important information.
3. Have paper, pencils, and calendar ready for use.
4. Know your schedule before you start making appointments. It is unforgivable to make an appointment with a potential buyer when you already have an appointment.
5. Know exactly what you are going to say before you call.
6. Have answers ready for all possible objections.
7. Assume the attitude that you will secure the interview.
8. Rehearse your approach for at least five minutes before you make your first call.
9. Arrange interviews in one geographic area on one day and in another area on another day. Do not arrange appointments so that you have to leave one area, go to another, and possibly return to the first location at a later time during the same day.
10. Set a definite number of persons to call and call at definite times.

Prestige referrals

Many salesmen are trained to get a minimum of three prestige referrals from each client at the close of a sale. They are encouraged to get referrals throughout the year by giving good service to the client. Getting a referral is not getting a name— there is a great difference. Some salesmen get names, while others get referrals. Some salesmen obtain several referrals, while others seldom get one referral.

A salesman in Detroit who came to me with prospecting problems doubled his sales when I pointed out that *getting referrals* was his weakness. I showed him how much business he would have secured by getting three referrals from each client. He had been selling for three years but had not known how to ask for referrals. We practiced one entire afternoon on getting referrals from the prospects in his markets. At the end of the session, he was proficient in obtaining every type of referral that he needed. He doubled sales immediately, just by solving this one problem.

In the life insurance industry, life underwriters work with a strong referral known as a power lead. Ben Rocca, Jr., of Occidental Life Insurance Company, San Jose, California, works almost exclusively with power leads.

Ben says, "For a great many years we have used the system of 'power leads.' This method is known to many successful people in the industry and to many successful people in other industries. What is a power lead? You might, in a sense, say it is the tremendous power of names.

"If we in the business of life insurance were to call on a busy executive as 'Ben Rocca, Jr., and Associates', we probably would get a stock answer, 'Not interested.' However, if we call on the same executive as 'Ben Rocca, Jr., and Associates' in the business of life insurance, introduced by his closest friend or biggest client or stockholder, we would undoubtedly get the result that our prospect would immediately stop everything he was doing, invite us in, and listen to our story most attentively."

Ben adds, "In acquiring 'power leads' we always endeavor to seek out a person who has the relationship that will open the door of the person to whom we would like to talk. If we are thinking of a prospect in the medical profession and our prospect specializes in surgery, we are interested in finding a 'power lead' of another M.D. in the identical or a closely related field, such as another reputable surgeon who is a personal friend of our prospect and for whom our prospect will have a great deal of professional respect. The mind level of these two people, when thinking of each other, will be the same, due to their mutual associations and understanding.

"This type of prospecting can be applied to any business or profession and can also be very effective between employees as well as employers. Keep in mind that prospecting is observation! It is what you hear and what you see!"

Some companies have their salesmen ask for three references after each sale. The client gives three references, and they are just that—references, not referrals. When the salesman calls on the reference, it is, for the most part, as cold as if he had selected a name at random out of the telephone book.

Some salesmen ask for referrals in a tone that implies, "You don't want to give me any names, do you?" I suggest a "brain-storming" session on getting referrals at frequent intervals, until every salesman has made getting referrals second nature.

Direct mail

There are many types of letters that may be used as a pre-approach letter to soften the prospect for a telephone call. Some firms send direct-mail letters, offering a gift to the replier; some offer information; some offer an idea, but very few letters ever state that a salesman will call the prospect for an interview.

Here is one experience with a company which I shall call the XYZ Company of Chicago, Illinois. This company asked me to train their salesmen in telephone techniques. When I asked if they sent direct mail to potential buyers, the answer was that each salesman sent 1,000 letters each week. The sales manager confessed immediately that their results were poor and that the men wasted driving and waiting time to contact the prospect, who, upon many occasions, was not at home when the salesman arrived.

During the first session, we established goals and outlined a systematic plan of prospecting to follow for a period of time. I suggested to the group that we eliminate wasted money in postage on direct mail and reduce the quantity from 1,000 letters per man to 100 per man.

Most of the salesmen objected immediately. One salesman asked, "How can we get enough leads from 100 letters to keep us busy, if we don't get enough from 1,000 letters to keep us busy?"

That was a fair question. Also, the purpose of our sessions was to increase sales. On the surface it seemed like a ridiculous suggestion. However, when I quoted results from other similar firms that had combined their direct-mail system with a telephone system, the men agreed to reduce the quantity of letters from 1,000 to 100 per man.

During the past several years, the salesmen had obtained mailing lists of persons scattered over a wide area, without any attempt to select a particular market or area. We started using street directories from the Telephone Company, which enabled each salesman to work for some time in one particular area.

The lists had been sent to the home office for typing and mailing. We asked that the letters be returned for local mailing, along with the lists, so that we could follow up the mailing with telephone calls.

The salesmen had merely waited for reply cards to be returned to them. Then they called upon these persons with the gift that had been offered for each replier. In many cases the people were not at home and that meant a return trip for the salesman. In some cases, the persons were not potential buyers; they were not interested in the service or could not afford it. The results from previous mailings had been unsatisfactory, both in the cards being returned and in the number of sales from personal visits.

In some cases the nonreplier is the best prospect, but these salesmen were not calling on him.

This is the schedule we used for direct mail for the following weeks:

1. Each salesman mailed 100 letters the first week. He mailed 50 letters on one day and 50 on the following day.
2. Each salesman telephoned the first group seventy-two hours after the letters were mailed and attempted to get an appointment.
3. Each salesman then telephoned the persons on the second mailing seventy-two hours later and attempted to get an appointment. In this way the salesman did not have to spend a great deal of time on the phone on either day.
4. The salesmen arranged their appointments geographically, which saved considerable time in driving. Also, their prospects were at home waiting for them at the appointed time.

5. The salesman did not waste time in waiting for a reply card to be returned. He telephoned everyone and made the letter seem far more important than it had been previously.
6. The salesmen made more appointments and closed more sales from 100 letters than they had for 1,000 letters.
7. The second week we had to reduce the quantity of letters for the most experienced salesmen, as they were obtaining so many appointments they could not handle the business for 100 letters.

This is just one illustration of how a local mailing can be made extremely effective through the use of the telephone, proper timing, and proper organization.

Personalized letters

A personalized letter is one that is signed by your client, introducing you, your product or service to his friends, relatives, or acquaintances. It is a strong recommendation, if used to its greatest advantage.

The letter is general, short, simple, direct, with a brief introduction of you, your product or service. It states that the client has benefitted in some way from the use of your product or service and suggests that the recipient of the letter might also benefit, in some way, from your product or service. For example, if you perform a service, the general theme of your letter might be:

"John Jones recently performed an excellent service for me that has saved a considerable amount of time and money. As this service was of value to me, it might possibly be of some value to you."

The composition of this type of letter should be general in nature, as many persons are reluctant to sign a letter stating many specific benefits. The letter should introduce you by name in the first sentence. It should state some benefit received, with a mild suggestion that the recipient of the letter might also benefit from your service.

If you work with different markets, you might consider writing two or three different letters that would be applicable for your particular markets. A professional man would not sign a letter that had been slanted for a person who was in a low-income bracket; nor would a person in a low-income bracket sign a letter slanted for a businessman or a professional person.

If you are interested in using a personalized letter, I suggest that you test it in your markets. The results you get will indicate its value to you.

1. This letter is typed in advance by the salesman on plain white bond paper of excellent quality. The body of the letter is typed, leaving the remainder of the page blank.
2. Keep a minimum of twenty letters typed in advance, placed in your briefcase, unfolded, ready for signature.
3. After the completion of your sale or service, request your customary number of referrals. Some salesmen obtain a minimum of three referrals; others obtain as many as seven or eight. It depends on you!
4. After you have obtained the names and addresses of the referrals from your client, make a smooth transition to the letters and get a letter signed for each referral.
5. Take the signed letters back to your office and have your secretary or secretarial service type the names and addresses on the letters, according to the signature on each letter. The secretary can match the shade of typewriter ribbon on the name and address to that of the body of the letter.
6. Your secretary or secretarial service should type an envelope (plain, white, matching the paper) with the name and address of each referral and mail the letters.
7. Forty-eight hours to seventy-two hours later, you should make a telephone call to each referral and make an appointment.
8. Set up controls to determine your earnings from the letters..

Service calls

Sometime ago in Miami, Florida, I was discussing service calls and sales techniques with K. H. Hatling, branch manager of IBM Electric Typewriter Division, and his assistant, O'Brien J. Doyle.

Upon my inquiry as to the extent of service rendered in their business, Mr. Hatling said, "Selling is service in our business."

Here are some suggestions for keeping score:[2]

WEEKLY RECORD OF
PERSONALLY SIGNED REFERRAL LETTERS

Name	Date Mail.	Date Phoned	Date Appt.	Date Sale	Amt. of Sale	Commission Earned
1.						
2.						
3.						
4.						
5.						
6.						
7.						
8.						
9.						
10.						
TOTALS						

TOTAL NUMBER OF LETTERS MAILED WEEKLY   ———————

TOTAL NUMBER OF PHONE CALLS MADE WEEKLY   ———————

TOTAL NUMBER OF INTERVIEWS OBTAINED   ———————

TOTAL NUMBER OF SALES MADE   ———————

TOTAL WEEKLY PRODUCTION ON LETTERS   ———————

TOTAL WEEKLY COMMISSIONS EARNED ON LETTERS   ———————

AVERAGE COST PER LETTER   ———————

AVERAGE EARNINGS PER LETTER   ———————

---

2 "Weekly Record" is reprinted from *Tele-Teck Training Program* by Mona Ling.

Mr. Hatling added that service was stressed in every phase of their activities.

Mr. Doyle added that during the years he had been a salesman with IBM, he had personally given service to every customer.

Mark Twain once said, "People spend a great deal of time talking about the weather, but no one does anything about it." It has been my observation that many salesmen spend a great deal of time talking about service, but few salesmen follow through on service calls in a systematic way so as to increase their flow of prospects.

Karl Bach, insurance salesman extraordinary, of Penn Mutual Life Insurance Company, San Francisco, does one of the best jobs of keeping in touch with his customers of any salesman in the business. Karl telephones his customers wherever they are and invites them to call him collect, if they have any problems or questions.

In his book, *How I Sell $12,000,000 of Life Insurance Year after Year* (published by Pacific Books, Palo Alto, California), he tells of one incident that occurred in receiving a collect call from a customer.

A young man purchased a modest life insurance policy from Karl, and soon after he became a Naval officer. From time to time, this man or his wife telephoned Karl from various parts of the country to ask a question or to make an inquiry about coordinating their insurance to the retirement and pension plans made available to servicemen by the government.

One day Karl received a collect call from this man in the East. After a brief chat, the wife came to the telephone and said, "Incidentally, Karl, my husband just got a big promotion. We want a $100,000 policy on him and $10,000 each on me and the children." This incident is just one of many large sales that have resulted from Karl's keep-in-touch policy.

Wayne Frey, eastern district sales manager, Crompton & Knowled Packaging Corporation, also saves a lot of service time through the effective use of the telephone.

Mr. Frey said, "I'm no different from other salesmen who are constantly called on the telephone by customers who have a problem or who want me to perform a service. But over the years I have learned to handle these requests in a minimum of time. When a customer calls me, I immediately ask what his problem is, and then, in a nice way, I transfer the call to someone else who can handle the specific request.

"Sometimes a customer will ask me to come out to his plant. Depending on what he wants to discuss, I have someone else in my office get on the telephone with me to go over the problem. Usually it turns out to be simpler than the customer realized and can be handled right at the moment. I kill a lot of potentially time-consuming service requests by using the telephone to its fullest advantage." [3]

Ebby Halliday, prominent realtor in Dallas, Texas, said recently: "With the market tightening and our inventory increasing, we have realized more than ever the value of keeping in touch with each homeowner; servicing his listing by a weekly personal visit to review with him the specific activity (or lack of it) on his property and to discuss the market in general.

"We also keep in close touch by telephone. It's amazing how regular reports, initiated by the listing salesman, can lay the groundwork for (1) an extension of the listing, (2) a possible price reduction, (3) an offer, (4) perhaps some fresh paint and repair, (5) in many instances a trade, exchange, or owner assistance in financing, (6) to say nothing of the far greater possibility that you will make another sale."

Ebby added, "Find what else the home owner has to sell. I almost passed up a big ranch listing this year by hurrying away with a signed contract of sale on an owner's home. It had been a difficult price negotiation, and my tendency was to take my signed contract and run. I remained to give a brief outline of my service and, looking for a pleasant departing comment, I remarked on a ceramic replica of a fine bull on the mantel, which led to an animated conversation about his ranch and to its sale

---

[3] Reprinted through the courtesy of *The American Salesman*, April, 1962.

within six weeks' time. This residential sale led to a half million dollar ranch sale!"

Fred Jenkins, prominent realtor in Cedar Grove, New Jersey, told me recently that giving quality service was the major phase of their activities. Fred said, "We keep in constant touch with our clients and keep them informed of our activities and progress. We believe the telephone is the greatest tool in the possession of a salesman, regardless of what he is selling."

TIPS FOR EFFECTIVE PROSPECTING

Charles L. Lapp, Ph.D., professor of marketing at Washington University, trains over 100,000 salesmen each year. The suggestions for effective prospecting are based on Chuck's ideas expressed in his classes at the University and in his numerous workshops that are held throughout the United States and in other countries. Chuck is the author of *Successful Selling Strategies* and *How to Outsell the Born Salesman* (distributed by Business Book Company, 7162 Pershing Avenue, St. Louis 30, Missouri.)

1. Be prospect-minded.

Be prospect-minded and grow with the growing industry with which you are associated. This is in no way meant to indict those salesmen who have worked hard to assist their dealers to be better merchandisers. Typically, however, a salesman over a period of years can't depend upon increased sales through established accounts to take care of his future.

2. Do some prospecting every day.

Many salesmen phone or call on established accounts and often never have time left to do any prospecting, while other salesmen have disciplined themselves to make a certain amount of calls each morning.

3. List periodically the accounts in your territory that you aren't selling.

Periodically, sit down and list the accounts in your territory you are not selling. At this point, don't say to yourself, "I tried to sell this one or that one for three years, and it is hopeless." Remember conditions change and the unapproachable prospect of yesterday may be an easy one to sell today. Check to find out if conditions have changed! Possibly the prospect has a new purchasing agent, an establishment has a new owner, or an establishment that didn't stock some item is now doing so in a big way. Then, too, no matter how well a competitive salesman services an account, there is always the possibility that the salesman's company associates have done something to antagonize a buyer. When a competitive salesman is replaced in your territory, it is particularly an opportune time for you to step up your prospecting activity.

4. Develop a prospect plan.

Develop a prospect plan by being on the lookout for leads in your own territory that may mean additional business:

Businesses to be opened
Changes in management

Follow up on leads obtained or sent to you by your sales manager:

Catalog requests
Market surveys
Convention leads
Advertising leads
Trade publications
Association bulletins

Develop new prospects by consulting:

Industrial directories
Newspapers
Chamber of Commerce lists
Telephone directories

Remember, that even the best salesman sometimes loses an account. Your best bet for replacing these lost accounts is in an up-to-date, well-kept prospect file.

5. Use your contacts to tip you off on prospects.

The salesman's natural interest in people makes him gregarious.

His ability to make friends and hold them is truly an asset. Local business and professional men represent your market, so get acquainted with them. Within the limits of reason, time, and bank account, be a joiner; take your place in community affairs, both business and social. Extend your circle of acquaintances beyond those who are themselves potential customers. You are in competition with other salesmen. To know what is going to happen before it happens is an advantage. Often this can be accomplished by enjoying friendly relations with those on the inside track. Who is the top salesman in your town? He's the fellow who "knows everybody," who is on speaking terms with everyone from elevator starters to bank presidents. Widen your circle; win friends by being a friend.

6. Evaluate the time you should spend on prospecting.

Many salesmen don't spend enough time on prospecting. However, it is possible to spend so much time that you lose established business through the neglect of accounts. Prospect with an objective. If in gaining a larger account, you lose a smaller account, it still is profitable for a salesman. If, however, the reverse happens, then a salesman's time would not be well spent.

7. Classify prospecting accounts.

Classify prospective buyers and determine how many calls each may be worth, based on the probable volume if you should crack the account. Also, you might well list or check off accounts on what you feel to be a probability basis of making repetitive sales. Then, too, some prospects may be small buyers now, but you should ask yourself this question, "Is there a possibility that they will be big buyers in the future?" You can often grow with an account, when you can't crack it after it becomes a big buyer.

8. Don't assume that you can't make an appointment or sale on the first call.

Never assume that you can't make an appointment on your first telephone call, or a sale on your first personal visit. Statistics may be against you, but some salesmen are proving the statistic-grinders wrong every day. Don't be discouraged if you don't make an appointment on the first phone call, or a sale on the first personal call. Some buyers want to make certain they give their business to someone who is going to be around and who, too, will appreciate their business. A good axiom to follow is: "Cultivate gradually, but don't hound."

9. Use all means of prospecting.

All prospecting does not have to be done by means of a personal call. Some of your prospecting can be done by mail or telephone. It is not very likely that an account will be sold by mail or telephone, but these means may be used to get an appointment, qualify a prospect, and possibly do something to "soften" him up so that he might be sold with *fewer* personal calls.

10. Keep your eyes and ears open for prospects.

There are a number of ways prospect leads may come to you, but you must keep your eyes and ears open. Market opportunities, as businesses expand, are daily made available. The business notes of local papers may give you a lead. A competitive salesman may drop a remark that indicates a lead. Remodeling of facilities may indicate a demand that previously may not have existed. Constantly watch for shifts in channels of distribution. Also, salesmen, in the opinion of some experts, have too much of a defeatist attitude toward the possibility of selling certain types of distributors or industrial accounts.

11. Prospecting calls may be on established customers.

Prospecting calls, particularly by mail or telephone, may not always need be on new prospects. There may be some line you are trying to sell. A suggestion by mail or by telephone may be enough to sell a number of your accounts on a minimum inventory of an item you might suggest to them. Then, too, your present customers may give you a lead and entrée to new business, if you have helped them in some significant way.

12. Make certain on a prospecting call you are talking to the right person.

When making a telephone call, make certain that you are talking to the right person. Often an employee, or even a partner in a business who does not buy or who has no authority to buy, will take up a lot of your valuable time and listen to you. If there are a number of employees, it may be well to ask directly, "Do you have authority to buy?" If they don't, be cordial and follow up by asking, "Is there any way that I might be of assistance to you?" The person may not be able to make a commitment for a purchase but still have considerable power in recommending.

13. Make a check-up on your prospect presentations.

Make a check-up on your prospect presentations when you fail to get results. Ask yourself, "What do my regular customers accept that a prospect who has said 'no' doesn't accept?" An effective salesman must be a prospect getter, a prospect seller, as well as a business builder with established accounts.

14. Answer all questions in a prospect's mind.

According to Jack Lacy, who for years has been outstanding in his clinics for salesmen, there are five questions that must be answered in any prospect's mind before a sale and a customer can be made out of a prospect. The prospect may or may not be conscious of these questions. The questions may exist only subconsciously. These five questions are as follows:

Why listen?
What is it?
Who says so?
Who has bought it?
What's in it for me?

You may find, even though a prospect doesn't audibly ask all or any of the above questions, that if you answer them, a prospect will be more receptive to you and your proposition.

15. Make prospecting a part of your regular sales activity.

Make prospecting a part of your regular sales activity and you will find it will pay off handsomely in increased sales over a period of time. Don't be discouraged your first day of prospecting, your second day, or the first week, or the first month—the payoff comes from your cumulative efforts.

Chuck says, "Try a prospecting plan based on these fifteen

suggestions. Keep track of the time you spend on prospecting activities and see if you are not handsomely rewarded for your efforts."

KEEP SCORE BY RECORDS

Establish a systematic prospecting system, selecting the best methods suitable for your product or service. Set up a time-control chart, utilizing your working hours to your greatest advantage. Set production goals in advance and make a breakdown by the day, week, month, and year. Determine the number of telephone calls you have to make, based on your ratio of appointments to calls, and the number of interviews you have to make, based on your ratio of sales to interviews. Arrange a consistent work pattern, so you can make the required number of calls and interviews. You can then control your production scientifically.

A monthly prospecting and production control chart will enable you to keep score on your direct mail, prestige referral calls, cold calls, appointments obtained, cases opened, and cases closed.

Make use of properly designed control records to determine whether you are doing a constructive job in prospecting activities. Review these records to determine your weak points so you can correct them. A control record is a planning tool. It enables the salesman to economize his time, plan his work, conserve his energy, and it serves as a record of his performance. A carefully designed and properly executed control record will make a valuable contribution to the salesman's career and his success.

MONTHLY PROSPECTING & PRODUCTION CONTROL CHART [4]

DATE	DIRECT MAIL RECORD				PRESTIGE REFERRALS			COLD CALLS			TOTAL			
	Quan. Mail	No. of Calls	No. of Appts.	No. of Sales	No. of Calls	No. of Appts.	No of Sales	No. of Calls	No. of Appts.	No. of Sales	Con-tacts	Appts. Obt.	Cases Opened	Cases Closed
1st Wk.														
Total														
2nd Wk.														
Total														
3rd Wk.														
Total														
4th Wk.														
Total														
5th Wk.														
Total														

TELE-TECK ORGANIZATION CHART

Ask yourself the following questions to determine your strong and weak points of organization. Assign a value of five points to each *yes* answer. Those questions that you answer *no* will show your weak points.

	YES	NO
1. Do you have cards, lists, and numbers ready before phoning?	___	___
2. Do you have paper, pencils, and calendar ready?	___	___
3. Do you make calls at the best time?	___	___
4. Do you follow letters with phone calls?	___	___
5. Do you systematically obtain referrals from clients?	___	___
6. Are you prospect-minded?	___	___
7. Do you do some prospecting every day?	___	___
8. Do you list the accounts you aren't selling?	___	___
9. Have you developed a consistent prospecting plan?	___	___
10. Do you use your contacts to obtain prospects?	___	___
11. Do you evaluate the time you should spend on prospecting?	___	___
12. Do you classify accounts based on possible volume?	___	___
13. Do you assume that you will make appointment on first call?	___	___
14. Do you use all means that you know in prospecting?	___	___
15. Do you keep your eyes and ears open for prospects?	___	___
16. Do you prospect at times with established customers?	___	___
17. Do you make certain that you are talking to the right person?	___	___
18. Do you make a check on your prospecting presentations?	___	___
19. Do you answer all questions in a prospect's mind?	___	___
20. Do you make prospecting a part of your sales activity?	___	___

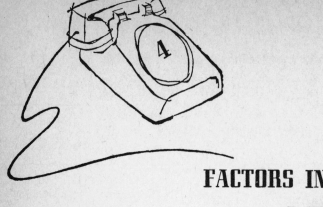

IMPORTANT FACTORS IN DEVELOPING A PRESENTATION

If a man empties his purse into his head, no man can take it away from him. An investment in knowledge always pays the best interest.

BENJAMIN FRANKLIN

ONE OF THE FIRST requisites of prospecting by tele-phone is to have an effective presentation. The development of a presentation is dependent upon many factors:

1. Knowledge of product
2. Awareness of what people buy
3. Buyer attitudes and behavior
4. Principles of selling and closing
5. Telephone techniques

Of equal importance is the ability to organize knowledge, materials, ideas, and to construct them into a meaningful pattern.

The success of an effective presentation is dependent upon the physical and mental attributes of the salesman:

Friendliness	Speech
Enthusiasm	Voice
Attitude	Listening
Willingness to serve	Visualization
Creativity	Effort
Personality	Ability

The quality of the telephone call is dependent upon the effectiveness of the presentation, the effort, ability, and adaptability of the salesman.

PRODUCT KNOWLEDGE

One of the first requisites of selling is product knowledge. "Know thoroughly what you are selling and be sold on it yourself before you try to sell it," says Anthony P. Zifcak, franchised agent for General Development in Providence County, Rhode Island, and winner of nine *New York Times* awards for best classified advertising in a New England newspaper.

"Know what you are selling," was echoed by salesmen in many industries: vacuum cleaners, furniture, insulation, specialties, chemicals, paint, jobbers, wholesalers, home improvement, automobile, insurance, securities, real estate, tools, equipment, machinery.

Elmer G. Leterman, one of America's greatest salesmen, says, "The more you know about your job, the more it will take possession of you; and the more it possesses you, the more your enthusiasm will ring and sparkle in every word you speak of it."

The same is true of your product. The salesman who knows all about his product can find many ways of selling it, or of getting appointments to sell it.

List the benefits of your product (or service) on a sheet of paper, then ask yourself these questions:

1. What are the most attractive benefits?
2. How can I translate these benefits into terms my prospect will understand?
3. What sales or advertising materials do I have in my files that will aid me in writing my presentation?
4. What is the key message of my presentation?
5. How can I give the key message in one sentence?
6. What personal experience can I use to help me illustrate my message, if necessary?
7. Who uses my products?
8. Who has benefited from my products?

WHY DO PEOPLE BUY

One of the most important requisites in selling is learning why people buy. Buyers have one thing in common; they all desire to satisfy a want, need, craving, or inner drive. Sometimes people themselves are not aware of these wants until salespeople arouse their desires and bring them to their attention.

People normally make purchases because they believe that the ownership of the products will grant them some degree of benefit. This is true, even when the motivating force may be pride of ownership rather than use value.

Most buying motives are emotional in nature, and nearly all consumer goods and services are sold through appeal to the customer's basic pride. Most consumer purchases are made to satisfy one or more of twenty-five buying reasons:

1. To make money.
2. To save money.
3. To save time.
4. To avoid effort.
5. To gain comfort.
6. To achieve cleanliness.
7. To improve health.
8. To escape pain.
9. To be popular.
10. To attract the opposite sex.
11. To gain praise.
12. To conserve possessions.
13. To increase enjoyment.
14. To gratify curiosity.
15. To protect family.
16. To be in style.
17. To satisfy appetite.
18. To emulate others.
19. To have beautiful things.
20. To avoid criticism.
21. To take advantage of opportunities.
22. To be individual.
23. To avoid trouble.
24. To protect reputation.
25. To have safety.

These twenty-five reasons for buying can be grouped into seven basic reasons. Most successful sales result from an appeal to one of these basic reasons. What are they? Prestige, love, imitation, fear, curiosity, rivalry, and self-preservation.

Prestige

It is a fundamental characteristic of all people to desire to raise themselves in the eyes of other people. There is a tendency to measure success by what other people think. One of the quickest and easiest ways to develop prestige (in the eyes of your neighbors) is through the ownership of valuable or unusual goods. "Keeping up with the Joneses" is no longer the American way of life. Now it's "passing the Joneses" that counts.

Love

One of the most effective sales appeals is love. Parental love makes it difficult for parents to refuse any desires within reason that their children may express. People buy items for children's health, amusement, education, comfort, etc.

Romance is another segment of the love motive that is responsible for millions of dollars' worth of sales each year. This appeal is valuable in selling many products, from luxury items to housewares.

Imitation

Imitation is another strong reason why customers buy products. How many of us buy a new car because the one we have will absolutely not run another mile? Not many of us. The deciding factor here is how many new cars there are in our neighborhood, or whether our best friend just bought a new eight-cylinder, high-compression Magnifico convertible.

If you saw someone looking skyward, you too would probably turn eyes upward. There is nothing strange about this action. Imitation is common to all mankind.

Fear

We all dread the thought of fire, flood, famine, accidents, death, war, going without the necessities, and the like. This fear is a strong motivation factor that results in many sales. Insurance policies, preventive medicine, heating units, air-conditioning units, etc. are sold by using this motive.

In playing up the fear motive, the salesperson should describe to the customer what could happen if he continues on his present course. Then an explanation of how his product will protect him should be given.

Curiosity

It is a fundamental trait of human nature to be curious about something in which our interest has been aroused and has not been completely satisfied. If you have ever read an exciting mystery novel and were tempted to turn to the last page to find out what happens, you are familiar with the power of curiosity.

If you can arouse the customer's curiosity about your product, you will lower his sales resistance, keep his attention, and leave him wide-open for the rest of your sales presentation.

Rivalry

People like to excel others in what they are doing. If we can show customers how buying our product will help them excel others, we are on the road to making the sale. Because rivalry is not as strong a buying motive as some of the others, it is wise to supplement it with other basic motives.

Self-Preservation

The desire of self-preservation extends from personal care to the welfare and well-being of a man's family. In this respect it is closely connected with appeals to parental love and romance. The goods and services that are sold through this appeal are too numerous to mention.

It is not always easy to determine which of the seven basic appeals will be the most effective. Usually, it is a combination of several appeals that brings the desired results.

Depending on the reaction of each customer, the salesperson

should feel his way until he discovers which appeal, or combination of appeals, would be the most effective. The sales presentation can be built around this appeal.

"Why Do People Buy" has been reprinted through the courtesy of Charles E. Hersheway, editor-in-chief of the National Research Bureau, Inc., Chicago, Illinois. It was compiled by the editorial staff and originally printed in Volume III of *Retail Advertising and Sales Promotion Manual,* which is distributed by National Research Bureau, Inc.

Check your list of benefits and tie them in with what people will buy. For example, if your product saves your clients money, you would use that appeal in your telephone call, then later in your selling interview.

1. How can I best tie in the benefits to the wants of my prospects?
2. How can I present them in a new and different way that will evoke favorable response?
3. What are the basic needs of my prospects?
4. What are the basic wants of my prospects?
5. What is the primary interest of my prospects?
6. What are their secondary interests?
7. What appeal will be of the greatest interest to most of my prospects?
8. What specific facts can I use, if any are needed?

Jack Wardlaw, author of *Top Secrets of Successful Selling* (New York: Wilfred Funk, Inc., 1952) and *Inside Secrets of Selling* (New York: Fleet Publishing Company, 1958), says: "The basic task of the salesman is to find a need and fill it."

The essential message of his book *Inside Secrets of Selling* can be broken down into six simple words: find a need and fill it. This has been the motto of Jack Wardlaw through his selling career.

"Anyone who wants to sell, whether it be a product, a service, or just himself and his ideas, has to start with an understanding and appreciation of the needs of others. This is as necessary to the housewife or artist as it is to the Fuller-brush man, the grocer, or the corner druggist," says Jack, who is one of the nation's top salesmen.

PRINCIPLES OF SELLING

In your basic sales course you learned that all sales follow a definite pattern:

1. Attention
2. Interest
3. Conviction
4. Desire
5. Close

In selling, you may not follow these steps in this order, but you most probably will follow all five steps before a sale is successfully consummated.

In telephoning, your purpose is to sell an appointment. The basic rules for selling an appointment are the same basic rules as for selling a product. The difference is in your choice of words, your technique of selling the appointment, and the time involved. You probably will use a few hundred words, which will be spoken within three to five minutes, in selling an appointment. You might use a few thousand words in selling a product in an interview. The time might vary from thirty to forty-five minutes, to a couple of hours.

What is selling? Selling consists of reaching people's minds with an idea that will open their pocketbooks.

What is prospecting? Prospecting consists of reaching people's minds with an idea that will open their doors for an interview.

TESTED TELEPHONE TIPS

Here are a few suggestions for developing a telephone technique and for giving direction to your presentation, as well as a pattern or framework.

1. Introduce yourself and your firm.
2. State the purpose of your call.
3. Give your prospect a benefit from listening to you.
4. Give your prospect a benefit from granting an interview.

5. Offer a service, if possible.
6. Use a "hinge" or plausible reason for calling, such as direct mail, referral, or a personalized letter.
7. Stick to a central idea.
8. Stick to a central track.
9. Give the prospect choices.
10. If making a daytime appointment, ask for off-hours.
11. Make the appointment your sole objective.
12. Don't attempt to educate the prospect on the telephone.

In attempting to educate the prospect or to transact business, the prospect loses interest, and the salesman loses control of his prospect.

In asking for choices of time, you might practice the following and use those choices that are applicable to your markets and prospects:

"Which would be more convenient for you, the morning or the afternoon?"

"Which would be more convenient for you, the day or the evening?"

"Which would be more convenient for you, the first of the week or the latter part of the week?"

"Is the better time to see you in the morning, or would the afternoon be better?"

"Which would be better for you, the morning or the afternoon?"

"Which would be better for you, the day or the evening?"

"Which would be better for you, this morning at 10:30 or this afternoon at 2:20?"

After the morning or the afternoon has been established as the best time for the prospect, you might ask for choices of time:

"Which would be better for you, 9:20 or 10:40?"

"Which would be better for you, 9:40 or 11:20?"

"Which would be more convenient for you, 1:40 or 3:20?"

"Which would be more convenient for you, 2:20 or 3:40?"

The busy executive sometimes responds more readily to a request for an off-hour than he does to an appointment on the hour.

For the evening appointment, you might want to ask for a choice on the hour or half-hour.

"Which is better for you, 7:30 or 8:30?"
"Is an early hour better for you, or do you like to get the children to bed first?"

HOW TO EVOKE FAVORABLE RESPONSES

The telephone presentation should be designed to get the most favorable responses from the most people. Motivational research has shown that people buy benefits, not products; they respond to certain qualities in others, and to positive statements. The statements below are general and not conclusive.

1. People will respond more favorably to a positive statement than to a negative one. Advertising contains many positive statements. We know that "Coca-Cola is the pause that refreshes."
2. People will forget what you say but not how you say it.
3. People will respond more favorably if you adopt a "customer-you" attitude than if you talk about yourself.
4. People will respond more quickly to well-known brands or familiar names than to unknowns. People believe that "You can be sure if it's Westinghouse."
5. People will respond to specific qualities and colors. Women will buy more hosiery if you will change the color from beige to "Sundown" or "Desert Sand."
6. People will respond more readily if you give them choices than if you make all decisions for them.
7. People will respond more favorably and quickly when they feel a sense of fair treatment.
8. People will respond to a salesman who is friendly, courteous, and who expresses the utmost integrity in his manner and actions.
9. People will respond quickly if the salesman makes a good impression at the beginning of the telephone call. First impressions and most sales start at the telephone, therefore it is impossible to overestimate the importance of creating a good impression as soon as possible.

10. People will not respond favorably to commands, threats, rudeness, loud voices, deceit, or being forced into an appointment against their will. It is against human nature to be forced. "A man convinced against his will is of the same opinion still."

PROSPECTS LIKE FRIENDLY PEOPLE

A successful vacuum cleaner salesman said, "Friendliness is one of the most important personality traits a salesman can possess." He added, "People like to do business with friendly people."

This salesman once worked in Los Angeles, and during that time obtained eighteen referrals from one satisfied customer. He sold most of the eighteen persons vacuum cleaners.

Tom Hinckley, of Equitable Life Assurance Society, believes that *naturalness* is one of his greatest assets. Tom is friendly but has a naturalness that puts prospects completely at ease.

"When I talk to a referral or a client, I try to establish a feeling of ease, comfort, and friendliness. Most salesmen want to talk, but I've discovered that people relax more, open up more, if I let them talk. They also feel more at ease." Tom said, "When you can get someone to talk about himself, you are on your way to an appointment or a sale."

ENTHUSIASM IS A HIGH-PAID QUALITY

Bruce Barton once said, "If you can give only one gift to your son or daughter, let it be enthusiasm."

I have met many salesmen who lacked polish or finesse, who did not know a great deal about sales techniques, but they sold products. They made sales because they were so enthusiastic about their product or their idea that they generated enthusiasm in the prospect.

Sometime ago I attended the Western New York Accident and Health Association's Health Insurance Sales Congress in Buffalo, where several dynamic speakers stressed the importance of being enthusiastic in order to influence the prospect's immediate reaction. The speakers were: Oakley Baskin, J. F. Crozier, John English, Charles Kingston, and Frank Bettger.

Frank Bettger, by his own admission, was a failure in selling, but lifted himself to the top by discovering the importance of being enthusiastic. He tells about his experiences in his book, *How I Raised Myself from Failure to Success in Selling* (Englewood Cliffs, N.J.: Prentice-Hall, 1949).

Frank said, "Force yourself to act enthusiastic, and you'll become enthusiastic. Make high resolve that you will double the amount of enthusiasm you have been putting into your work and into your income, and double your happiness."

He asked, "How can you begin? There is just one rule: 'To become enthusiastic, act enthusiastic.' Enthusiasm is the highest paid quality on earth!"

A great American industrial statesman, Clarence Francis, once said, "You can buy a man's time, you can buy a man's physical presence at a given place, you can even buy a measured number of skilled muscular motions per hour or day, but you cannot buy enthusiasm!"

In my Sales Workshops throughout the United States and Canada, many hundreds of men and women have given telephone approaches for the purpose of practice and evaluation. These approaches are given exactly as they would be on the telephone. Many of the persons had no enthusiasm at all in their voices, manner, or thoughts.

When a salesman says, "Mr. Smith, I have a great idea I'd like to discuss with you," his voice should reflect the fact that he has a great idea. When this statement is made in a drab, colorless, monotonous voice, it has no effect on the prospect. He doesn't believe it is a *great* idea.

When a salesman who is filled with enthusiasm says, "Mr. Smith, I have a great idea I'd like to show you," the prospect believes the salesman has a great idea, and he will react to the enthusiasm in the salesman's voice and manner.

Enthusiasm is just as important in making a telephone call as it is in making a sale—perhaps more so. The enthusiasm in your voice goes out over the wire to your prospect, evokes interest, commands attention, gives vitality and motivation to your presentation. Enthusiasm gets action!

PROPER MENTAL ATTITUDE

Early in his experience, Sid Flanders, of London Life Insurance Company, Montreal, Canada, found himself going through a prolonged "dry spell." He realized that he could easily get caught in a vicious circle of "no business" because of his attitude and letdown feeling. Sid told himself that everybody likes to do business with successful people.

Though it was difficult in the beginning, he decided that he had to assume success. He had to become an actor, which took a lot of application and self-discipline. He started to dress like a successful life underwriter; to think, talk, and act successful. Soon this assumed attitude had a magic effect, not only on prospects and clients, but on himself. He really started to believe he was successful. It was easy to believe when his commission statements showed good results.

"Nothing succeeds like success," says Sid, "and an attitude of success that is assumed for a period of time will one day become a feeling of success." [1]

Dorothy Belz, of General American Life in St. Louis, said, "The right mental attitude results from what the salesman thinks about his work, clients, company, and even himself. What the salesman thinks affects his attitude, and his attitude creates an atmosphere of failure or success."

The right mental attitude at the telephone will increase appointments. Many successful salesmen think that attitude is more important than ability at the point of the phone.

A salesman in Cincinnati said, "When my sales slump and my telephone calls are not effective, I check my attitudes. Most of my problems in prospecting and selling seem to stem from my attitudes."

[1] Used by permission of *Canadian Insurance* (Toronto, Ont.: Stone & Cox, Ltd., 1962).

Here is a checklist to determine whether your attitudes are affecting your phone calls:

		YES	NO
1.	Did I have the attitude that I was going to get the appointment?	___	___
2.	Was my attitude one of interest in the prospect?	___	___
3.	Did I listen to him?	___	___
4.	Did my attitude reveal that I liked the prospect?	___	___
5.	Was my attitude that of a professional salesman?	___	___
6.	Was my attitude that of a successful salesman?	___	___
7.	Did I concentrate on what I was saying?	___	___
8.	Did I communicate my ideas effectively?	___	___
9.	Did my attitude reveal confidence?	___	___
10.	Was my attitude optimistic?	___	___

SERVE AND SELL

One of the most important keys to effective telephoning is to offer a service to the potential buyer. After the sale, give quality service to the buyer.

Elmer Leterman says, "Give your client as much attention after you've sold him as before."

The telephone enables salesmen to give better service to clients than ever before. Charles F. Johnson, editor of Dartnell's Sales Executive's Service, reported this incident in a recent report:[2]

The Eglin Air Force Base in Florida had urgent need for 100 feet of 2-inch by 3-inch flat bars. Not just any kind of steel; it had to be a special alloy for making bomb bands. The procurement officer called many sources of steel from coast to coast. Nobody had the type of steel needed, in the size specified, and in the amount required. The officer then called the United States Steel Supply Division's district sales office in Birmingham, Alabama. "Would Birmingham, by chance, happen to have a supply of the special alloy?" "No," said the district sales manager, his warehouse did not stock that highly specialized item. But he didn't let it drop there. A bare possibility existed that the quantity needed

---

[2] Reprinted through the courtesy of The Dartnell Corporation, Chicago, Illinois.

might be found in another U. S. Steel warehouse somewhere in the United States.

Within a few hours, Eglin was informed that the bars it needed were in a U. S. Steel warehouse in St. Louis. Now the only problem was speedy delivery to Florida. That, the Air Force explained, would be easy. A cargo plane would be dispatched to the nearest airport. "Fine," said the U. S. Steel district sales manager in St. Louis. A company truck with the steel will be waiting at the edge of the airport. By midnight, a C-47 was heading back to Eglin with its ton of steel.

A willingness to serve clients is at the top of the list of successful salesmen.

A woman was interviewing a prospective butler for a position. "How do you serve?" she asked.

"Both ways," the butler replied.

"What do you mean 'both ways'?" she asked.

The butler replied, "So they'll come back, or so they won't."

A salesman can serve "both ways"—so his clients will buy more, or so they won't.

CREATIVITY

Three days before his death in a plane crash, Mike Todd spoke to the student body at Royce Hall, UCLA. Mike said, "A great salesman must do three things to be successful: (1) sell fearlessly, (2) never run out of ideas, and (3) never look back."

Mike Todd was a great showman and a great salesman, who practiced what he preached.

This is the age of the idea salesman and the idea salesman is consistently the top producer in his firm. The potential power of creative ideas is limitless. Many ideas call for unconventional thinking; for man to get off the beaten path, to be different, to explore new ways of doing things better.

If you want to become more creative, use your imagination. Albert Einstein said, "Imagination is more important than knowledge."

A salesman must have knowledge, but knowledge alone will not make a man a great salesman. The salesman who uses his imagination will achieve greater results than the salesman who does everything the same way he did it five years ago.

John Dewey said, "There is no label, on any given idea or principle, that says automatically, 'Use me in this situation'—as the magic cakes of Alice in Wonderland were inscribed 'Eat me.' The thinker has to decide, to choose, and there is always a risk; so the prudent thinker selects warily, subject, that is, to confirmation or frustration by later events."

To perfect a skillful telephone technique requires creativity. The salesman dials a number of his own choice, introduces himself to a stranger, and asks for an appointment. The stranger resists this suggestion. The salesman proceeds to arouse interest and create desire for his product; he skillfully overcomes objections; he wins the confidence of the prospect and persuades him to grant an interview. All of these things take place within three minutes.

I have no scientific proof that the skillful use of the telephone will increase the salesman's creativity, or his imagination. But my findings have shown that the salesman who develops a skillful telephone technique becomes more proficient in his other skills. He learns to communicate with others more creatively and effectively; he develops listening skills and increases mental alertness. He often increases sales within hours, not weeks, and closes more sales more quickly, skillfully, and effectively than he did prior to the development of a telephone technique.

Many men and women have increased their sales to 30 per cent after one Sales Workshop and maintained that increase until completion of the workshops. After the completion of a program, I have no access to sales records, therefore cannot know the results over a long period of time. Some participants have increased sales up to 55 per cent. It depends on the individual, his wants, desires, goals, and objectives.

Alfred North Whitehead said, "We must beware of what I call 'inert ideas'—ideas that are merely received into the mind without being utilized, or tested, or thrown into fresh combinations."

LISTEN AND SELL

Someone once said, "Great talkers are like leaky vessels: everything runs out of them."

"Too many salesmen are poor listeners," says John Croxall, of Mutual Fund Associates in San Francisco. "Too many salesmen think they have to keep talking, both on the phone and in the interview.

"The salesman who engages in active listening can draw the prospect out and find out how he likes to be treated as a person. He can find out what the prospect thinks, how he feels, and how he responds.

"The salesman who talks but doesn't listen frequently overtalks. The salesman who overtalks loses appointments and sales." John said, "Listen more and sell more."

Long before the development or growth of salesmanship as we know it today and long before the invention of the telephone, Plutarch said, "The talkative listen to no one, for they are ever speaking. And the first evil that attends those who know not how to be silent is that they hear nothing."

As listening is the weakest of the basic communication skills and yet is one of the most important, this subject is discussed in a chapter with many suggestions for improvement.

PERSONALITY PAYS

Ralph Clingaman, Michigan state manager of Midwestern United Life, said recently in a sales meeting: "The development of a good personality is a tremendous help to a salesman. The salesman's friendly personality creates interest and releases strain in the mind of his prospect. A good personality will greatly improve a salesman's chances of getting appointments."

Dr. Georgette McGregor, lecturer in effective speech and public speaking at the University of California, Los Angeles, said, "Personality is usually defined as a concept or organization of a large number of traits in an integrated pattern. Another way personality can be explained is that personality is how an individual looks to others. In your daily life, what impression do you make on others?"

"Like electricity, personality is difficult to handle because we see what it does and how it works, but it is not possible to know completely its fundamental nature. We do realize that success in almost every line of endeavor depends upon an ability to make a favorable impression on possible clients or customers. The impression made is what is called personality."

Dr. McGregor believes that "Personality can be measured a great deal by attitudes. It is obvious that negative attitudes will attract negative results. On the other hand, positive attitudes will result in more pleasant outcomes. Personality grows as character is strengthened. Weakness of character is often failure to cultivate the self and to develop personality.

"Personality emerges when an individual begins to understand the meaning of his behavior as it affects him and as it is interpreted by others. Why is it we like people? Here are a dozen reasons why we like people:

1. Like cheerful people.
2. Like natural people.
3. Like dependable people.
4. Like tactful people.
5. Like people who build up our self-esteem.
6. Like people who make us feel important.
7. Like people who let us talk.
8. Like people who do not try to reform us.
9. Like people who are adaptable.
10. Like friendly people.
11. Like understanding people.
12. Like people who like us.

"It is an exceedingly narrow view that knowledge plus hard work equals success, because personality figures into the picture so strongly. There are certain traits without which, even though you have plenty of ability, skill, brains, and information, you can scarcely expect to succeed in competition with other men and women." Dr. McGregor says, "These traits include ambition, persistence, patience, dependability, industriousness, forcefulness, self-confidence, effectiveness of speech, consideration, tact, cheerfulness, friendliness, naturalness, and adaptability."

When asked, "Why do you buy from that salesman?" people invariably answer, "He has a nice personality."

The salesman who develops an interesting and pleasing personality finds that it pays, and pays, and pays!

SPEECH HABITS TRAIN THE MIND

Effective speech has been defined as bigger and better conversation. Effective speech includes sharing of ideas, feelings, moods, and information. Wherever you are, or whatever you do, you cannot do without speech.

Good speech habits can train the mind in many ways. Efforts to speak well force an individual to clarify his thoughts, to strike out the irrelevant, to synthesize materials, to subordinate minor points, and to state his message without waste of words.

"Speech is man's greatest invention," said Irene Wilson of Cosmetics by Irene, Inglewood, California. "Good speech always secures and holds attention. If you do not hold attention in a telephone conversation, check your speech habits.

"The first thing to learn about speech is how to stop. It is as important to be able to stop talking as it is to speak convincingly."

Irene gives suggestions for effective speech habits:

1. Don't overtalk.
2. Translate your speech for the prospect.
3. Choose wording carefully.
4. Know what you are going to say.
5. Practice aloud.
6. Check for correct enunciation.
7. Check for correct pronunciation.
8. Be interested in what you say.

Dr. Georgette McGregor says, "The impressions you make depend largely upon the vigor with which you talk, the tact with which you express your ideas, and the pleasantness of your voice.

"Here is a recipe for a potent personality cocktail, which serves as an excellent catalyst when working for more effective speech:

⅔ Knowledge, poise, and charm
⅓ Sense of humor, tact, and cheerfulness
Add a generous dash of appreciation for others.
Mix well, serve in generous portions, and reap the happy results."

Pronunciation of words is extremely important in effective speech; however, the salesman must learn quickly how to pronounce the prospect's name. In order to learn how to pronounce the prospect's name, the salesman must be sure that he heard it correctly and repeated it correctly. If you are in doubt, you can easily check the spelling against the following list. Learn this list so that you can use the name you wish instantly.

A—Alice	N—Nellie
B—Bertha	O—Oliver
C—Charles	P—Peter
D—David	Q—Quaker
E—Edward	R—Robert
F—Frank	S—Samuel
G—George	T—Thomas
H—Henry	U—Utah
I—Ida	V—Victor
J—James	W—William
K—Kate	X—X-ray
L—Louis	Y—Young
M—Mary	Z—Zebra

YOUR VOICE IS YOU

Whether it is service, good will, or reputation, when you talk on the telephone, your voice is you, your firm; and the impression it makes today may influence your sales tomorrow.

"Many salesmen's voices advertise to their prospect, 'I'm not worth listening to, so don't waste your time on me,'" said Greg Whitaker, of First United Life, Fort Wayne, Indiana. "Other salesmen give a completely different picture through a controlled, well-modulated, pleasing voice.

"Many salesmen have dull, uninteresting, colorless voices only because they don't know they have them," Greg added.

"My men and I were certainly surprised to hear how we sounded. We were working on telephone approaches and put them on a tape recorder. We played the tape back, and the results were pretty bad. Since that time we have frequently set aside a part of our meeting to give attention to 'how we sound to our prospects.' During the week we work on simple exercises to give us a more interesting voice."

Check your voice against the questions below, and set aside some time to give serious thought and study to voice improvement.

1. Is your voice weak?
2. Is your voice too loud?
3. Is your voice too harsh?
4. Is your throat tense?
5. Is your voice monotonous?
6. Is your voice too nasal?
7. Is your voice shrill?
8. Is your voice affected?
9. Is your voice colorless?
10. Is your voice irritating?

Set aside definite times each day for correct voice work and improvement.

VISUALIZE YOUR PROSPECT

Dorothy Walters, West Coast advertising executive and author of *The Selling Power of a Woman* (Prentice-Hall) was reminiscing one day about her first lesson in the business world.

As a young girl she was thrilled to be employed by the Classified Advertising Section of a large Los Angeles newspaper in their Voluntary Department. This meant her job was taking on the telephone incoming ads that people "volunteered." The girls were given prizes if they could persuade the people to place their ads for a "7"-time, or "30"-time contract. Dorothy caught on to the sales talk quickly and was delighted to see her name climb to the top of the list.

Then their star saleswoman returned from her vacation. She sat down at the desk next to Dorothy, adjusted her headset, and left Dorothy in a cloud of dust. At first Dorothy couldn't figure out what had happened. She decided to keep her eyes and ears open and her mouth shut. She became an observer of this "pro" who sold more ads than anyone else in the entire department.

Here are some of the things this excellent saleswoman did:

1. She closed her eyes while she was talking. In her mind she visualized her customer, his needs, his problems, and she gave him her full attention.

2. She remained seated quietly without dissipating her energies in moving around and in using nervous gestures. She lowered her head so her mouth was close to the mouthpiece and spoke directly into it. Her voice went out over the wire with calm, controlled tones.

3. She had a beautiful voice, with good articulation; clear, resonant tones, with perfect pacing and timing. She did not speak in a monotone, but gave movement and vitality to every sentence.

4. She asked questions of her customers rather than telling them her sales talk. She was courteous when the customer talked and listened attentively to every word.

5. Her voice was sincere and so was her smile. Warmth and friendliness were transmitted over the wire. She seemed to talk with her heart and not just with her mouth.

Dorothy says, "Your telephone is the front door of your business." She ought to know. Dorothy started a business with a typewriter on two old orange crates, an idea, and enthusiasm. She made contacts from door to door until she could afford a telephone. Her business now employs over 130 people, who make over 3,500 calls each month. Hospitality Hostess Service handles over 1,500 advertisers with hostesses in forty-eight communities. It is the largest business of its kind in California.

Visualize your prospect and speak directly to him. Speak to him as if he were seated across the desk from you. This visualization will enable you to speak in a natural tone of voice. Many persons raise their voice when they talk on the telephone because they know the prospect is some distance away.

EFFORT TIMES ABILITY

Ned Spring, president of the Spring Company and Spring Company Florida Sales in Minneapolis, is a dynamic and vibrant person, who takes a very active part in the management of his organization. In choosing his staff, he makes it quite plain that each man will be given responsibilities, and that he is in charge of that segment of the business that is charged to him.

Donald Wagner, vice-president in charge of the Florida Sales Division, is also a dynamic, forceful person, who is always thinking of new ways to increase sales volume. If one idea doesn't work, he will discard it and use another approach.

The one formula that Don drums into his salesmen, however, is the very basic theory of $E \times A = R$, or Effort times Ability equals Results. He explains it this way: "Each man has a certain amount of native ability. If he uses all of this ability and couples it with a 10 per cent effort, his results will be far from his maximum capacity. Likewise, if a man exerts a maximum effort but has very little innate selling ability, his results, too, will be far from the optimum peak. But the man with a medium amount of selling ability who applies 100 per cent of his effort to his job will show results that would be a credit to any of us."

This thinking works! It has worked for many years for many salesmen in various industries, and it will work for salesmen everywhere.

Elmer Leterman says, "What turns the ordinary into the extraordinary is the extra you put into it."

HOW TO WRITE
A PRESENTATION

The difference between the right word and the almost right is the difference between the lightning and the lightning bug.

MARK TWAIN

YOU HAVE reviewed the benefit of your product or service and have listed the most attractive benefits and have tied them in with what people buy. Your next step is to write the presentation so it will:

1. Gain attention.
2. Arouse interest.
3. Convince.
4. Create desire.
5. Get action.

Write your presentation so it will gain certain responses when you give it to the prospect on the phone:

1. Response of approving.
2. Response of thinking.
3. Response of feeling.
4. Response of acting.

The basic purpose of all communication is to gain some sort of response from another person. To get favorable response from another person, you should be able to express your ideas clearly.

66

WORDS ARE IMPORTANT

The ability to express ideas is fully as essential as the capacity to have ideas. In making a telephone call, the impact you make depends largely upon your ability to express yourself in a language that is easily understood. Words are tools. Weigh them for maximum motivation. Through the use of the right words, you will be able to gain attention and an appointment. Each group of words is strung together like a series of beads, linking your thoughts to one central idea. Every word is important to that idea. The close correlation between a successful presentation and a skillful use of words should influence you to select words with great care.

Words in relationship to the buyer's response have been under the microscope for years. We know the buyer's behavior is to a considerable extent influenced by the choice of the salesman's words. Naturally, the words you select are determined by your product, benefits, service, and prospects.

Here are some general suggestions that will assist you in the writing of your presentation.

Do's

Use short, simple, uncomplicated words.
Use the present tense as much as possible.
Use words that create a mental image.
Use words that the listener doesn't have to translate.
Use words that appeal to the senses and basic needs.

Don't's

Don't use general, complicated, technical words.
Don't overuse or abuse certain words.
Don't overuse *I—Me—My*.
Don't use words with ambiguous meanings.
Don't use slang, colloquialisms, or foreign words.

Ten most expressive words

After years of research, Dr. Wilfred Funk and his staff have given us the ten most expressive words in the English language.

The warmest	—Friendship
The gentlest	—Tranquillity
The most tragic	—Death
The saddest	—Forgotten
The most bitter	—Alone
The most revered	—Mother
The most comforting	—Faith
The most beautiful	—Love
The most cruel	—Revenge
The coldest	—No

CAPSULE COURSE IN HUMAN RELATIONS

Someone once wrote a capsule course in human relations, giving the importance of words:

5 most important words—I am proud of you
4 most important words—What do you think
3 most important words—If you please
2 most important words—Thank you
1 least important word —I

This capsule course in human relations is golden advice and, when heeded, brings wonderful results.

PHRASES

The business of writing a presentation is the business of making choices between words and between arrangements of words. When writing a telephone presentation, trust your ear, not your eye, because the presentation will be heard, not read. Select *spoken* words and arrange them into attractive phrases.

Use familiar phrases that make the prospect feel comfortable and that give him something to compare your idea with in his everyday life. Select phrases that build an image and appeal to the senses: shape, colors, movement, warmth, smoothness, sounds.

Avoid trite, tired, overworked phrases, such as—"Is that so?" . . . "I know what you mean." . . . "Sure enough" . . . "You're telling me." . . . "Well, what do you know."

Avoid bookish phrases when a simple word or two will express your meaning.

Instead of:	Say:
along the lines of	—like
for the purpose of	—for
for the reasons that	—since
from the point of view of	—for
in as much as	—since
in accordance with	—by
in the case of	—if
in the nature of	—like
in order to	—to
on the basis of	—by
with a view to	—to
with reference to	—about
with the result that	—so that
likewise	—and
furthermore	—besides
nevertheless	—but
that is to say	—in other words
more specifically	—for example
to be sure	—of course
for this reason	—so
accordingly	—and so
consequently	—and so
hence, thus	—therefore

SENTENCES

In making outgoing calls, your prospects are nearly all unwilling listeners. You dial a number of your choice and introduce a subject of your choice. In some cases the listener has never heard of you, your firm, your product, or service. Therefore, your sentences should be constructed so that your listener can easily understand your message.

1. Construct your sentences in the order in which the listener will use the information and can understand it. Simplicity and clarity are essential in the writing of a presentation.

2. Arrange your key words and phrases so that they will be heard by the listener. On the average, the listener remembers only about one-tenth of what is said; therefore, you want him to remember important words and phrases.

3. Keep sentences short. They should vary in structure and length but, on the average, be short, and express one idea.

4. Avoid long sentences that express two or more ideas. If you use a long sentence, keep it as simple as possible. Use a control element, such as "however," etc. For example, many salesmen use long sentences with a control element in their answers to objections to make a switch from an objection to an advantage. "I can appreciate that a man in your position would be busy; *however*, other busy men have told me this idea saved them both time and money." There is an effective pause at the word "however" to give the prospect an opportunity to make the change in ideas.

5. Avoid unnecessary words and phrases. Your sentence should show clarity, directness, and conciseness. It should get the message across to the listener with the least amount of energy on his part.

6. Write your presentation with one person in mind. Don't think of dozens or hundreds of persons who will hear it. You will give it to one person at a time so write it with one person in mind.

7. Use terms your reader can picture. Visualize the benefits as you write your presentation. If you can't visualize them, your listener probably won't be able to either.

8. Write the way you talk. Write your presentation and read it aloud to determine whether it sounds like conversation or a presentation being read.

Express your meanings in concrete, unambiguous terms. "Reasonable men," says Beardsley Ruml, "always agree if they understand what they are talking about."

PRESENTATION

We live in a world in which no two persons are alike in every respect. We cannot generalize and say that one presentation will appeal to all prospects. We can say that a well-prepared presentation will have far greater results with prospects than an unprepared presentation. Our purpose should be to write a presentation that will appeal to the most people and get the best results.

If we are to work maturely, we must be aware of both the similarities and differences in people and train ourselves to adjust to those similarities and differences. A great deal of your adaptability comes through the delivery of your presentation and your "feedback" mechanism. Your presentation serves as a springboard to get into a conversation with your prospect. As you listen to your prospect, you will make use of what he says and how he says it, making changes in vocal delivery as the conversation progresses, and in the use of words. Most of the adaptability of a salesman is made in rate of speech, in timing, pacing, inflection, intonation, and in vocal expression.

LOGICAL SEQUENCE

If your presentation follows a logical sequence, it will produce better results. This logical sequence has been used by many successful salesmen. It is given here merely as a guide.

Your first step in most cases is to determine whether you are speaking to the proper person or not, then proceed:

1. *Name of prospect.*
2. *Your name.*
3. *Name of firm.*

4. *Courtesy request.*

5. *Repeat prospect's name.*
6. *State idea or benefit.*

1. "Mr. Smith,
2. . . . this is Bill Jones,
3. with the Ajax Air Conditioning Company.
4. Have you a moment to speak on the phone?"
   (Wait for reply.)
5. "Mr. Smith,
6. I'm calling to tell you about our new air conditioner that fits right into the window of any room in your home and doesn't require any installation. Our air conditioner can be moved from room to room very easily, which increases the comfort of the entire family. It's economical to own and homeowners tell us there is a considerable saving in money, plus the convenience of being able to use it where it is needed most.

7. *Minimize time of interview to make time attractive to prospect.*	7. It will take fifteen minutes to show you and Mrs. Smith the many advantages of our new air conditioner; then you can determine its value to you and your family.
8. *Ask for appointment.*	8. Which would be a better time for you and Mrs. Smith to see this air conditioner, the day or the evening?"

ROAD-MAP FOR PHONE CALLS

Ford salesmen use a "road-map" for phone calls that serves as an excellent guide. This "road-map" is printed on a 3 x 5 card so the salesman can carry it with him at all times. The comments under number 4 in qualifying the prospect would naturally change with the product, equipment, or service.[1]

1. *Identify party you are talking to.* (This saves time.)
2. *Take Off-Curse.* (Do you have a moment to talk to me?)
3. *Tell your name and dealership.* (If you sent postcard, ask if it was received.)
4. *Qualify.* (Are you interested in buying a new car?) [Author's comments: "You have a (make and year of car) don't you, Mr. Smith?" "How many payments do you still have left to make?" "I think we could refinance your payments right now so you'd be driving a brand-new Ford for less than you're paying now. If I could do that, would you be interested in buying a new Ford?"]
5. *Appointment.* ("What time?" Set a certain time. Remember you can't sell a car over the phone.)
6. *Call-back appointment.* (When may I call you again.)
7. *When a prospect?* (May I put you on my prospect list?)
8. *Referral.* (Whom can I sell a car to today?)
9. *Set up for bird dog.* (Do you have a pencil, and will you write my name down on the front of your telephone book?)
10. *Service lead.* (Sell your dealership.)
11. *Send follow-up postcard.* (Keep contact alive.)

---

[1] "Road-map" reprinted through the courtesy of the Ford Motor Company.

Here are some general ideas for telephoning that are taken from my recording *How to Get Appointments by Telephone.*[2]

"Jack Edwards, a mutual friend of ours, tells me that you're in the market for a new car. Is that correct?"

"Mr. Brown, has anyone assumed the responsibility of your automotive needs?"

"I mailed a letter to you last week that can save your firm considerable money. Did you receive it?"

"My firm has developed a specialized investment service that is proving very popular with businessmen in this city. I'd like to give you a free booklet and tell you about this service."

"My purpose in calling is to request the courtesy of seven minutes of your time to point out the highlights of my service."

"My company has designed a specialized plan for men in your profession that can increase the benefits of your program from 10 to 40 per cent without any additional cost to you."

"Your neighbor, Bob White, tells me that you're interested in buying a home near the high school. Is that correct?"

"My company has designed an unusual savings program for executives in your business."

"My company has developed an unusual service that has been of tremendous value to business owners such as you."

"My company has an idea that can give complete protection to your entire plant and decrease your present costs. You are interested in cutting costs, aren't you?"

"Mr. Stewart, I have an idea that would increase the effectiveness of your business without additional cost to you. This idea has been used successfully with several companies similar to yours. It will take twenty-two minutes for me to show you how this was accomplished. Would the morning or the afternoon be more convenient for you?"

"Mr. Thomas, this is Bill Jones, of XYZ Company. Recently I performed a service for Power Manufacturing Company that saved them a considerable amount of money. Dick Johnson was so pleased with the service and the saving that he asked me to get in touch with you. You are interested in saving money, aren't you?"

---

2 General ideas through the courtesy of Success Motivation Institute, Inc.

Select the general ideas that appeal to you and that are applicable to your benefits and write your presentation, using the logical sequence.

GETTING INFORMATION FOR FUTURE USE

Many salesmen obtain information for future use. Some salesmen who sell auto insurance make calls to uncover prospects.

"Mr. Roberts, I am making a survey for the Ajax Insurance Company. Would you mind telling me what make car you own at the present time?"

After obtaining this information, the agent asks about the insurance, when it expires, and other pertinent information. He keeps this information in his file for future reference and follows up with a telephone call at a certain time prior to the expiration date of the policy.

Auto salesmen frequently obtain information from car owners in advance.

"Mr. Wilson, I am making a survey for the automobile dealers of the metropolitan area. Would you mind telling me what make of car you drive?"

After the first question is answered, the salesman proceeds to other questions. Here are some of the questions that are asked in this type of survey.

Name of owner?
Address?
Number of cars?
Make of car now owned?
Where purchased?
Year of car?
Miles driven per year?
Is car used for business?
Is car used for pleasure? Both?
Considering a new car at this time?

Dr. G. Herbert True, lecturer and special consultant to many companies, said: "If your knowledge is not in order, the more confused you become. The less you know about a subject, the more you talk."

If you know your subject, clarify your thoughts, write your presentation the way you talk, and you will get your message across to the listener.

TELE-TECK CHECK LIST FOR AN EFFECTIVE PRESENTATION

Ask yourself the following questions to determine the strong and weak points of your presentation. Assign a value of ten points to each *yes* answer. Those questions that you answer *no* will show the weak spots in your presentation.

		YES	NO
1.	Did I use short, simple, uncomplicated words?	___	___
2.	Did I express my key message so it could be understood?	___	___
3.	Did I avoid trite, overworked, and bookish phrases?	___	___
4.	Did I maintain a "customer-you" attitude?	___	___
5.	Did I give the prospect a benefit of interest to him?	___	___
6.	Did I minimize time or make it attractive?	___	___
7.	Did I ask for a choice of "which or which" in time?	___	___
8.	Did I ask for an appointment instead of hinting at it?	___	___
9.	Did I stick to a logical order in the presentation?	___	___
10.	Will my presentation arouse interest and get action?	___	___

HOW TO GET
APPOINTMENTS
BY TELEPHONE

It makes a great difference in the force of a sentence whether a man be behind it or no.

RALPH WALDO EMERSON

SOME TIME AGO Elmer Leterman, one of America's twelve greatest salesmen, interviewed Arthur "Red" Motley, another of America's twelve greatest salesmen. This was an exclusive interview for the *Ford Dealer Magazine*. Elmer asked this master salesman to tell Ford salesmen what his advice would be if he were in the automobile business today. His reply was typically enthusiastic:[1]

"Nothing approaches the automobile business in excitement and thrill because, regardless of whatever sociologists may claim, the automobile is still one of the average American's most prized possessions.

"This can be a big year for the car salesman, but it will be big only because of your own efforts, not anyone else's. Here's how I would go about making it that way.

"I'd first try to create the proper climate. Nothing can contribute as much to your success, and to the success of those associated with you, as the climate that you create. What you believe in your heart is mirrored in your face every day of your life. Be sure the face you wear in your place of business, the face that is seen by those around you and by those you hope to sell, is one that inspires confidence.

"Remember that today news is the most salable commodity in the

[1] Reprinted through the permission of the *Ford Dealer Magazine*, Dearborn, Michigan.

world. Today more people read newspapers than anything else in print. Today they want to know more about what goes on in their areas, as well as in the world around them. But most of all, remember that you have news, too. Big news. The news is about your product—its fine styling, excellent performance, models tailored to suit, the trouble-free operation provided by warranty, new heights in quality—many more.

"Then there is another element to this proper selling climate. It is called tender loving care. What is tender loving care? It's the kind of care that keeps your customers coming back . . . makes each customer feel welcome . . . makes him feel protected and important. Do not make any promise unless you intend to keep it," says "Red" Motley.

"Red" Motley has given several suggestions that will sell cars or make appointments to sell cars:

fine styling
excellent performance
models tailored to fit
trouble-free operation provided by warranty

COLD CALL

If a salesman knows that a man owns a car that is not giving good mileage, he might open his remarks with:

Salesman: "Have you heard that the Falcon delivers up to thirty miles per gallon?"

Prospect: "Yes, I'd heard it, but I didn't believe it."

Salesman: "How many miles do you get with your present car?"

Prospect: "Oh, about ten, I guess . . . for city driving."

Salesman: "Would you be interested in a car that gives you up to thirty miles per gallon?"

Prospect: "Yes, if I liked the performance."

Salesman: "That's exactly how I would feel, Mr. Smith. An experienced driver knows that performance isn't just acceleration. It's the way a car handles, rides, and feels—and this is where Falcon is ahead. You'll have to drive the new Falcon to see that it is ahead in performance as well as economical in gas mileage. I can have a new Falcon at your front door within twenty-two minutes. Would that time be convenient, or would a later time this evening be more convenient?"

Prospect: "In twenty-two minutes is OK."

Salesman: "Thank you, Mr. Smith. I'll see you at seven twenty-two."

EXAMPLE—COLD CALL

Salesman: "Mrs. Cook, this is Bill Snow, with the Middletown Painting
and Decorating Company. The purpose of my call is to let
the homeowners in your neighborhood know that we're giving a 25 per cent discount on our services at this time. This is
so we can keep our men busy during a slack season and won't
have to lay any of them off. Tell me, Mrs. Smith, how long
have you owned your home?"

Prospect: "We've lived here over fifteen years. We were one of the
first families to move into this neighborhood."

Salesman: "I can appreciate why you've lived there so long, Mrs. Smith;
it's attractive and all of your neighbors keep their homes
painted and looking nice. May I ask how long it has been
since you had your home painted?

Prospect: "It's been about seven years, or more."

Salesman: "I'm glad I called you, Mrs. Cook. You could have your
home painted at this time at a considerable saving. You
probably are interested in saving money on it, aren't you?"

Prospect: "Yes, we're always interested in saving money whenever we
can. But you would have to talk to my husband."

Salesman: "I'd be glad to talk to him, Mrs. Smith. What time does your
husband get home from work?"

Prospect: "He gets here around 5:00 o'clock. We usually get through
with dinner around 7:30."

Salesman: "7:30 will be fine with me. Thank you for your courtesy,
Mrs. Smith. Good-by."

REFERRAL CALLS

The logical sequence for a referral is similar to that on a cold
call. One suggestion is to use the name of your referral as soon as
possible.

1. *Name of prospect..*	1. "Mr. Johnson,
2. *Your first and last name.*	2. . . . this is Jack Sweeney
3. *Name of firm.*	3. with Sweeney's Ford.
4. *Use prestige referral.*	4. You and I haven't met; however, we have a mutual friend in Dick Snyder, one of your neighbors." (Wait for reply.) (Make appropriate comment.)

5. *State idea or benefit.*

5. "Dick is fine, Mr. Johnson. He just bought a new Falcon from me and was so pleased with the fine performance and gas economy he felt you'd be interested in seeing one, too.

6. *Minimize time or state specific time.*

6. It will take twelve minutes to get a new Falcon over to your office so you can see for yourself why Dick is so enthusiastic about it.

7. *Ask for appointment.* (or demonstration.)

7. Would that time be convenient with you, or would a later time this afternoon be better?"

EXAMPLE OF REFERRAL CALL VARIATION

1. *Name of prospect.*

1. "Is this Mr. Harry Wilson?"
(Reply is "Yes.")
"Mr. Wilson,

2. *Your name.*

2. . . . this is Art Hughes.

3. *Name of referral.*

3. You and I haven't had the opportunity of meeting; however, we have a mutual friend in Frank Watt, one of your good suppliers."
(Wait for comment.)

4. *Courtesy request.*

4. "Frank is just fine. Do you have a moment to speak to me, Mr. Wilson?

5. *Give firm idea.*

5. Frank told me that you were planning to expand your business within the next few months. Is that correct?"
(Reply is "Yes.")
"I'm glad to hear that. Frank didn't say anything about your plans or your financial situation, but we find that most men who plan a major expansion program find themselves in need of some kind of financing. My firm, the ABC Company, has been able to help many other businessmen in this city to expand their businesses without any worry about money.

| 6. *Minimize time.* | 6. It will take about an hour to show you our services and how a confidential financial arrangement can be made. |
| 7. *Ask for appointment.* | 7. Which would be more convenient for you, the morning or the afternoon?" |

DIRECT MAIL

The purpose of sending a letter to your prospect is to acquaint him with your name, firm, product, service, or idea. A well-written sales letter will have a tendency to make the prospect more receptive to your phone call and to reduce resistances.

The formula for writing a sales letter is interest, desire, conviction, and action. Your letter should arouse interest by appealing to one or more of the seven basic reasons why people buy. It should create a desire to know more about it. Your letter should make your idea sound convincing, so the prospect will feel it is to his advantage to listen to you when you call. Your letter should stimulate the prospect to some kind of action.

The best days for a prospect to receive mail are Tuesdays, Wednesdays, and Thursdays. The best time to follow up on direct mail is within forty-eight to seventy-two hours after it has been mailed. The prospect should have time to receive the letter and read it, but not time to forget it.

Your telephone call will depend on the type of letter mailed to your prospect. Some letters introduce a benefit, idea, ask a question, offer a gift, or request that a reply card be returned.

Some general topics are:

"Would you like to reduce your car payments?"

"Would you like to use a set of creative selling books FREE for seven days?"

"Would you like to receive one year consultation service FREE?"

"Would you like to be more popular with the opposite sex?"

"Would you like to cut your office overhead 30 per cent?"

"Would you like to receive a new crisp five-dollar bill FREE every morning for the next twenty years?"

"Return the enclosed card and receive our FREE gift."

"To effectively and rapidly expose your idea to as many people as possible, at the least expense, the telephone is the only answer," says Leon Simmons, top producer in the sale of mutual funds. Leon "dials for gold" and finds it. Leon Simmons is not only a top producer but is a popular author as well. He has written and produced films on telephone technique in mutual fund selling and has written a book on that subject. Leon's film and book *Dialing for Gold* are used for training mutual fund salesmen. The material on mutual funds is being reprinted through the courtesy of Leon Simmons.

Leon sends a letter to the potential buyer. Here is an example:[2]

MUTUAL FUND COMPANY

Any City—Main Street—U.S.A.

DEAR MR. GOOD:

Here is a current prospectus for our Mutual Fund. Our good customer, your brother, Jack, suggested sending this to you. We both think you'll find it helpful and interesting.

Later this week, I'll telephone to arrange an appointment with you and Mrs. Good, so I can explain this wonderful plan.

Mr. Good, I'm looking forward to meeting you and telling you all about our fine investment program.

Very truly yours,

/s/ SALESMAN SUPREME

P.S. Am enclosing a signed introduction card from your brother.

The final activity at this stage concerns the prospectus and the introduction card. Put both of them in an envelope with the note, and they're ready to mail. The note would probably be classified as a form letter, hence should be filed with the S.E.C., pursuant to Rule N-24B-1.

---

[2] Reprinted by permission of Leon Simmons from *Dialing for Gold*, ($2.00 for the booklet), 8600 Hillside Avenue, Hollywood, Calif.

NOTE.—This material is not to be considered an offer of sale or solicitation of an offer to buy any security. It has been prepared for sales training purposes only.

Allow time for delivery. That's when our friend the telephone comes into the picture. You can ask the qualifying questions in minutes, whereas hours are required in the hit-and-miss, run-across-town method. Not only is this better for you, but it's better for your prospect, and he'll appreciate your thoughtful consideration of his time.

And you've mapped out your "campaign" in systematic, sensible order because:

First—You have complied with Federal regulations by delivering a current prospectus before making an appointment for soliciting specific business from your prospect, or even interviewing him.

Second—By your letterhead and formal method of contact, you have let your prospect know that you sell a legitimate "service" and are not from some fly-by-night organization. He also knows by this time that you represent a reliable and reputable securities house or sales organization.

Third—You have extended the courtesy he has a right to expect, by asking for an appointment rather than barging in on him unexpectedly. People like to do business with courteous and considerate salesmen. (If you call him not later than one day after he receives your letter, your courtesy *for* him "will rub off *on* him." You will get to talk with him on the telephone, and you'll likely get the personal meeting you want).

Fourth—And perhaps the most important, you now have the golden opportunity to qualify your prospect quickly, and to determine whether you have a *live prospect* or just a *dead suspect*.

Be prepared

The art of qualifying must be practiced and practiced until it's so perfect that the answer your prospect gives you—whether it be "yes" or "no"—will be so true and accurate that you can regard it as gospel! This can be accomplished best by rehearsing your qualifying question over and over again until it's letter-perfect. You'll know in your own mind when you're ready to spring it.

Don't wait too long

Under no circumstances should you follow up your letter with a telephone call later than one day after your prospect receives his prospectus in the mail. Later than the day following is very unwise, since interest wanes and your prospect will most likely be cold . . . or at least cool to your proposition.

IN ALPHABETICAL ORDER

In alphabetical order, A—B—C equals 1—2—3. If you have followed the proper procedures and telephone promptly, you have also:

A. Avoided lost motion.
B. Valued your time.
C. Acquired a system of qualifying.

With those important steps organized, prior to the phone call, do this:

1. *Be courteous* when you get your party on the line. Be brief and directional in your questions. You want to know whether or not he is a good prospect.
2. *Talk customer benefits first and foremost.* Every prospect will have the feeling "what does it all mean to me?" Tell him you feel you have the answer to a wonderfully convenient and prudent method of investing for his financial future. Let the prospect feel your sincerity.
3. *Dominate the solicitation for the interview.* Let him know that you want to review the program in detail personally with him and his wife, so they can see if your plan can be tailored to their needs. Let him know you are interested in having them see if your plan fits their particular objectives and circumstances.
4. *Make him the hero and star!* And make him really feel it! Repeat your prospect's name many times over! Everyone loves to hear his own name spoken. There seems to be some magical quality in it. Just be sure it's pronounced correctly.

BE READY TO TALK

Don't call unless you can devote your entire attention to the conversation. Bone up on all the lead information you have about your prospect and talk to him—don't read or falter in your message. Talk to him—not at him. All set? Dial, and your conversation could go something like this:

MUTUAL FUND PRESENTATION

Salesman: "Good morning, Mr. Good. This is Mr. Supreme from the Mutual Fund Company. Did you get my letter and the prospectus that your brother suggested I send you?"

Good: "Yes, Mr. Supreme, . . . I have it right here, but no chance to get to it yet."

Salesman: "Oh, that's all right, Mr. Good. I understand how busy you are. Can you spare a few moments on the phone now?"

Good: "Sure, go ahead. I understand you have an unusual investment program to offer."

Salesman: "Yes, I certainly have. Would you open your prospectus to Page 29, Mr. Good?"

Good: "All right . . . I have it."

Salesman: "You see, Mr. Good, this is a sensible and logical investment opportunity. Notice the last column to the right, where it says percentage of total market value. Do you see it?"

Good: "Yes, here it is."

Salesman: "Mr. Good, this column shows you where your money is diversified and invested as of last October 31. For instance, notice the third industry listed under the heading of Foods. Would you circle it, please?" (Since Mr. Good is the president of a wholesale grocery business, we start with the foods industry, which is most familiar to him).

Good: "Yes, I have it."

Salesman: "Fine, now let's assume, Mr. Good, that you have $1,000 in our Mutual Fund. As an illustration, let's use this hypothetical list of companies. Your proportionate interest in General Mills would be two-tenths of 1 per cent. Or, out of your $1,000, exactly $2.00 is invested there. Here's another, Hershey Chocolate Company. You have a three-tenths of 1 per cent in Hershey's, so out of your $1,000 investment, you have a $3.00 interest in that well-known corporation. Notice all other prosperous food companies: National Biscuit, Quaker

Oats, Wrigley's Gum, and so on. You'll also notice, Mr. Good, that 2.5 per cent of your dollar is invested in the foods industry. The only risk you have of losing part of the $25 out of your $1,000 is for the food securities to decline in value. To lose the entire $25, all the food companies listed here would have to go into bankruptcy simultaneously! Do you follow me, Mr. Good?"

Good: "Yes, I see what you mean. These are certainly the top food companies in the nation. Does the same hold true for all the other companies and industries I see listed here?"

Salesman: "Absolutely, Mr. Good. Just take a look at all the other large and growing corporations that you enjoy a diversified and proportionate interest in. Successful companies like G.E., Westinghouse, U.S. Steel, Parke Davis, and many others. The really big ones! You'll find, by carefully studying the list, that this group of companies represents, in our opinion, a most wonderful cross-section of American industry packaged together. A package of very carefully selected companies that we feel has excellent growth possibilities—spreading the risk of market fluctuations over many, many companies and industries. In other words, Mr. Good, you've got your eggs in many, many baskets . . . not in just one, or even a few. You understand, though, that whether you have $100 invested, or $1,000, or even $10,000, you still have the same proportion or percentage of interest in each of these carefully selected corporations—this wonderful package of American earning power!"

Good: "Sounds interesting, and quite logical, too. But what kind of interest does the investment pay?"

Salesman: "Well, actually, Mr. Good, although the rate of continuity of dividends is not assured, a mutual fund pays a varying dividend instead of fixed interest. I'll explain all this and our sales charges in detail when I see you personally. You'll be interested in the sales charges, too; they're listed on Page 14 of your prospectus.

Now you begin angling for the interview

Salesman: "On Page 9 you will find a hypothetical or sample illustration of an assumed investment of $10,000 with dividend income reinvested and capital gains distributions accepted in shares."

Good: "Okay, I have it."

Salesman: "This sample table covers the period from January 1, 1946, to December 31, 1955. This period was one of generally rising common stock prices. The results shown should not be considered as a representation of the dividend income or capital gain or loss that may be realized from such an investment made in the Fund today. Such a program does not assure a profit or protect against depreciation in declining markets. But notice, if you will, Mr. Good, the total value of your $10,000 worth of shares at the end of the period. Do you see the actual performance under the 1955 total value, Mr. Good? Isn't it wonderful?"

Good: "I sure do. Over $23,000. Looks wonderful! Wish I had known about this ten years ago!"

Salesman: "If you are reasonably certain in your own mind that this wonderful investment program is everything I've indicated it to be, Mr. Good, are you in a financial position to take advantage of our plan *now* . . . even on a small scale?"

Good: "Well, I'm committed to certain obligations at the moment, and won't have any money for investing until they're paid off or otherwise taken care of."

Salesman: "That's certainly understandable, Mr. Good."

Good: "Besides, I'd like my wife to hear the program, too. I think she has a right to be in on this. Would you mind coming over to the house and explaining it to her in a few months?"

Salesman: "Certainly, anything you say. But why don't we set up a luncheon appointment for this Wednesday, with your wife as my guest also . . . and if it's agreeable with her, we can start with say $300 and a small minimum investment plan, say $50 monthly to begin with, then increase it later as you are able.

Good: "No, I'm afraid that's too soon. The luncheon idea would be fine and would save your having to make an evening call, but I want to wait and start it with a more substantial amount. Let's hold off getting together for a while yet?"

Salesman: "I realize, Mr. Good, that $50 monthly is not the plan you would establish as a permanent investment program, but it would at least break the ice and let you get started in the right direction."

Good: "No, I'd rather not do that. When I start I want to do it right or not at all. In two or three months I should be ready, if the little lady agrees to quit spending so much and helps me set something aside."

Bow out gracefully

Agree with your prospect that he knows best; thank him for his time and put him down on your calendar for another call in about two months. However, don't just leave it there. Your job isn't finished yet!

Salesman: "There's one favor I'd like to ask of you, Mr. Good. I'm sure you have friends or associates who would be very grateful for this information. Whom can you think of that could be helped by such a wonderful service?"

Good: "Well, off-hand, I can't think of anyone. But if I do, I'll let you know."

Don't be fluffed off

Help your prospect in thinking *for* you and *with* you.

Salesman: "How about your office manager, or your plant foreman?"

Good: "No, my office manager just got married, and he's building a new house. He's strapped financially. My plant manager is getting along all right though. I pay him about $8,000 a year, plus an annual bonus. He should make a good prospect."

Salesman: "Fine, what's his name, Mr. Good?"

Good: "Jim Carlton."

Salesman: "And his age?"

Good: "Jim's about thirty-six, I believe."

Salesman: "Does he own his own home or rent?"

Good: "He owns a nice little place over in Maple Groves; bought it under the GI bill a year or so ago."

Salesman: "I see . . . and how about children?"

Good: "He has two—Jimmy, Jr., the same age as my brother's little boy, and he's seven. A little girl came along last Christmas time, I've forgotten her name."

Salesman: "That's a lot of help, Mr. Good. Does Mr. Carlton's wife work?"

Good: "Yes, about one night a week. She was a registered nurse and still tries to keep up on her profession."

Salesman: "That makes sense . . . Before I forget it, what's their address in Maple Grove?"

Good: "129 Eastwood, I think. Better check the phone book on that though."

Salesman: "I'll be sure to do that, Mr. Good. Now, about your own relatives . . . your aunt, or uncle, or your parents? Do you
think they'd be interested?"

Good: "No, I doubt it, but I'll tell you who might be . . . my
brother-in-law . . . if you can get his wife to listen."

The qualifying question

This short question will *make* or *break* the "immediate" possibility of a sale. The question must be asked only *after* you have
laid the groundwork for it, as illustrated in the preceding dia-
logue.

"If you are reasonably certain in your own mind that this wonderful
investment program is everything I've indicated it to be, Mr. Prospect,
are you in a financial position to take advantage of our plan *now!*
. . . even on a small scale?"

Leon says, "The telephone can play a major role in creating and
building your own financial future. It can be the lifeline of business—the difference between profitable success and a lifetime of
wondering—wondering why the breaks just never came your way."

PERSONALIZED CALL

The logical sequence of a call about a personalized letter is
similar to that of a call about a referral:

1. *Name of prospect.*	1. "Is this Mr. Thornton Woodson?" (Reply—"Yes, it is.")
2. *Your name and firm.*	2. "This is Robert Lewis, of National Business Services.
3. *Courtesy request.*	3. Do you have a moment to speak on the phone?" (Reply—"Yes, I do.")
4. *Repeat name of prospect.*	4. "Mr. Woodson,
5. *Mention referral.*	5. Jack Douglas, of the ABC Company, recently mailed a letter to you telling you that he had benefited considerably through my services. Did you receive the letter?"

(Reply—"Yes, but I haven't had time to call Jack to see what it was all about.")

6. *State idea or benefit.*   6. "That's the purpose of my call, Mr.

7. *Mention time.*   7. Woodson. It will take thirty minutes to show you what my services are, and how they have helped other men in businesses similar to Jack's and to yours.

8. *Ask for appointment.*   8. Which would be more convenient for you, the morning or the afternoon?" (Reply—"Morning.") "Would tomorrow morning at 9:20 be all right, or would Friday morning at 10:40 be better?" (Reply—"Tomorrow morning at 9:20.")

SERVICE CALLS

There are many different types of service calls. Your firm can suggest the best type for you to make in order to do the best job for your clients.

Some customer service calls that result in increased sales are made by stores.

"Mrs. Christian, this is Jane Doe with the Harris Furniture Company. Mr. Harris would like to invite you as one of our charge customers to come to our store on Monday or Tuesday for a preview of our store-wide sale that is being offered to the public on Wednesday. Which of those days would be more convenient for you?"

(Reply—"I think Monday would be all right.")

"Thank you, Mrs. Christian, we'll be looking forward to seeing you on Monday."

"Sell-A-Million" Sam Gross of St. Louis is considered one of the greatest buyers and promotion men in the industry of retailing. Sam recently retired after more than fifty years in retailing. Sam was a great showman as well as a great buyer and frequently staged promotional events that stimulated business, such as a six-day bike race, pet shows, swimming events, and a health center.

A great deal of his success can be attributed to his frequent use of the telephone. Sam and his employees would telephone customers and potential buyers and invite them to take advantage of their fabulous offers, events, or pre-sale promotions.

Sam was buyer of radios and sporting goods at Famous-Barr for over thirty-eight years. In addition to being buyer for radios and sporting goods, he became buyer for television and stereo records, auto accessories, cameras, and pet supplies for their downtown store and three branches. He was also chairman of the radio, TV, and camera buying divisions for all May Department Stores, an organization comprising more than twenty stores in ten leading cities.

Sam says, "I could not stress the effective use of the telephone enough. The telephone is one of the most useful and important tools to a person in any kind of business today."

TWO KINDS OF PROSPECTS

Your telephone calls will be made to two general kinds of prospects:

1. To qualified prospects.
2. To unqualified prospects.

For the most part, a salesman knows enough about his qualified prospects to secure the interview without having to ask qualifying questions; except in such a case as the interview on the phone that was conducted by Leon Simmons, who wanted to determine whether his potential buyer was in a financial position to take advantage of the investment at that time.

There is certain information that some salesmen should obtain from unqualified prospects. For example, an accident and health insurance agent would want to know the prospect's age, status of health, and possible ability to pay premiums before going on with the interview.

A salesman offering free rug cleaning to demonstrate a vacuum cleaner would want to know whether the woman owned a vacuum cleaner and what kind, when it was purchased, and whether she was satisfied with it or not. He would probably want to know how many rooms were carpeted, and other pertinent information.

A salesman making calls for home improvements would want to know whether the person owned a home, date of purchase, and other pertinent information before he went to the home for an interview.

PROFESSIONAL ATTITUDE

"Red" Motley said, in the exclusive interview with Elmer Leterman, "There is a difference between a pro and just another salesman. Take a look at everything you are doing as a salesman—review it. Find out why this or that worked, or did not work. You must accept the same fact that any other good professional man has to accept—*that you are never through learning*. After any training course in salesmanship, you must welcome more training. A real pro takes refresher courses and keeps up-to-date with every innovation.

"You can do the same . . . by practicing your salesmanship twenty-four hours a day, seven days a week. A professional salesman is a salesman all the time. He eats, sleeps, thinks, and thrills to the opportunity of being a 'want-creator,' which is the fundamental force behind all human progress." [3]

"Red" Motley's conclusion is: A professional knows that everything—his appearance, his mannerisms, the way he talks, the way he approaches everyone he meets—will add to or detract from his ability to *sell his product or service*. Knowing these things, the professional salesman will:

1. Analyze each failure to sell, to find the reason for that failure.
2. Submit himself to constant self-analysis and training to improve.
3. Always give "a little extra something."

"Because salesmanship is so fundamentally important to everyone in America, it deserves a professional attitude in every salesman."

---

[3] Reprinted through the courtesy of *Ford Dealer Magazine*, Dearborn, Michigan.

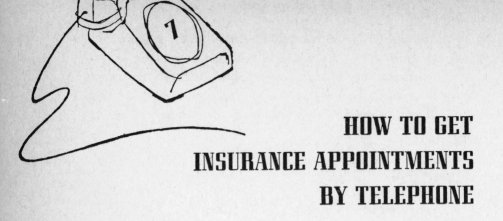

HOW TO GET
INSURANCE APPOINTMENTS
BY TELEPHONE

Quality is never an accident. It is always the result of intelli-gent effort. There must be a will to produce a superior thing.

JOHN RUSKIN

HUGH BELL, of Equitable Life of Iowa, Seattle, and I were discussing prospecting methods one day while having lunch at the Brown Derby Restaurant in Hollywood, California. I made the remark that many life underwriters who failed in the insurance business had plenty of ability, but just didn't know how to prospect. I asked Hugh if he believed there was a relationship between termination and prospecting. Hugh's reply was, "I have yet to see an agent leave the business who has solved his prospecting problems."

The insurance agent's position is unique, because he owes a high professional duty toward his client and prospect, while at the same time he also occupies a position of trust and loyalty with his company. His position demands the highest standards of performance in prospecting and selling. His conduct and performance, to a great extent, determine the public's opinion of insurance in general. The insurance agent is the one who establishes good public relations with the prospects and clients.

The agent who seeks to achieve success must establish a record of sincerity, honesty, and reliability. He must establish and formulate a constructive plan of representation in his community. He

92

must develop a method of prospecting that gives the impression of his being a truly professional person. The agents who achieve greater-than-average success almost invariably develop a system of prospecting by telephone. Through the use of the telephone, they develop skills in obtaining appointments, giving service, and promoting good public relations.

COLD CALLS

1. *Name of prospect.*	1. "Mr. Smith,
2. *Your first and last name.*	2. . . . this is George Knight
3. *Name of firm.*	3. with Midwestern United Life.
4. *Courtesy request.*	4. Have you a moment to speak on the phone?" (Wait for reply.)
5. *Repeat name of prospect.*	5. "Mr. Smith,
6. *State idea, service, plan.*	6. my company has designed an unusual savings and investment plan that has been of great interest to other men in your profession (or business).
7. *Minimize time.* (Fact-finding interview 7 to 12 or 22 minutes.)	7. It will take twelve minutes to show this plan to you and for you to determine whether or not it might be of value to you.
8. *Ask for appointment.*	8. Which would be more convenient for you, the morning or the afternoon?" [1]

George Knight usually obtains referrals but wanted to make some cold calls to develop his telephone skills. Within one week he closed three substantial cases from appointments he had made just practicing.

PENSION AND PROFIT SHARING

Monroe J. Beatty, of Aurora, Illinois, uses a question type of approach to get a commitment on a minor point. The sequence used is similar to that of George Knight.

---

[1] Reprinted through the courtesy of *Life Insurance Selling*, June, 1962.

1. *Name of prospect.*	1. "Mr. Jones,
2. *Your first and last name.*	2. . . . this is Monroe Beatty
3. *Name of firm.*	3. with Federal Life & Casualty.
4. *Courtesy request.*	4. Have you a moment to speak on the phone?" (Wait for reply.)
5. *Repeat name of prospect.*	5. "Mr. Jones,
6. *State idea, service, plan.*	6. you may or may not have heard of Senate Bill 804 that now allows members of your profession to incorporate for purposes of setting up a qualified pension and profit-sharing plan. The dollars contributed are before-tax dollars, not being subject to your normal income tax. In other words, the government contributes from 20 to 52 per cent of your retirement fund under this measure.
7. *Ask a question with a purpose that will progress presentation.*	7. You are interested in saving money, aren't you?" (Wait for reply. It will be affirmative, if the question was asked properly.) "The Internal Revenue Service is approving hundreds of plans weekly for men such as you.
8. *Minimize time.*	8. It will take twenty-two minutes for me to give you the highlights of this plan.
9. *Ask for appointment.*	9. Which would be more convenient for you, the morning or the afternoon?"

CALL FROM AUTO PHONE

Jack Wardlaw, of Raleigh, North Carolina, had a telephone installed in his car sometime ago. He drove around Raleigh looking at nice homes; then stopped in front of one. He called the owner on his telephone, introduced himself, and asked for an appointment.

The indignant man said, "I wouldn't talk with an insurance salesman on Sunday night, and, besides, I have company."

Jack said, "Well, there is no one in your driveway.   . . I am just out by your driveway."

The man rushed outside and got in Jack's car. He wanted to know all about the phone and how it worked. While Jack told him about the phone, he sold him a substantial amount of life insurance.

This unusual sale might have something to do with Jack's title of "U.L.U." (Unorthodox Life Underwriter).

REFERRAL CALLS

Most agents are trained to obtain a minimum of three referrals from each client when the sale is completed or when the policy is delivered. The agent who consistently obtains referrals never runs out of prospects.

Here is a short, simple approach that is used by Alfred Villasenor, of Penn Mutual Life Insurance Company, Los Angeles. Al does "nest" prospecting at several large industrial plants and sells over a million dollars of insurance each year with this simple approach.

> "Mr. Baker, this is Al Villasenor, of Penn Mutual Life Insurance Company. I've been exchanging valuable ideas with many of the engineers at your company, and though I haven't had the opportunity of meeting you yet, you have been recommended to me as a man who would be interested in my service. Would coffee on Tuesday or lunch on Thursday be better for you to see me?" [2]

Al has a warm, friendly, conversational voice. He instills confidence in the prospect immediately. He knows the coffee-break schedule for the various departments and the lunch schedule. At the time that I knew Al, most of his business was sold to employees of the industries where he had "nests"—centers of influence.

Ted Aronson, of North Miami Beach, Florida, works on a referral basis. Ted's calls are made to professional men for the most

---

[2] *The Insurance Field,* July 1960.

part, and 70 per cent of his cases are closed in his plush, well-organized office.

> "Mr. Jackson, this is Ted Aronson, a friend of Jim Brown. I am with the New York Life Insurance Company and recently did some rearranging with Jim's insurance and estate program. Jim thought it would be a good idea if I spoke to you along the same lines. He was amazed at how much more we were able to accomplish in extending his present coverage by the use of certain settlement options and consideration of an insurance trust. I would like very much to meet you to see if this service might be of interest to you. Which would be better for you, the morning or the afternoon?" [3]

Ted says, "Opportunity doesn't knock today—it rings!" He ought to know. Through effective prospecting by telephone, he qualified for the Million Dollar Round Table his first year in the insurance business. He has qualified for the MDRT each year since 1957. Last year he sold approximately $3,000,000. Ted led all New York Life agents in the twelve state Southeastern Region and was seventh in sales throughout the nation.

HEALTH AND ACCIDENT APPROACH

Charles Kingston and I met in Buffalo on the occasion of the Western New York's Accident and Health Insurance Sales Congress. Chuck was one of the principal speakers at the Congress. I was a guest of Howard Potter, of Empire State Life.

Later that day, Chuck, Howard, and I were talking about prospecting. Chuck said he operated exclusively upon a referral basis. His introductory telephone conversation is something like this:

> "Dr. Able, this is Charles Kingston. Doctors Baker and Charlie have said that I could use their names as a professional reference to you. Doctor Baker also informed me that he had suggested that you listen to me for a period of about twenty minutes, and that you expressed a willingness to do so." (Wait for comment.)
>
> "I would very much like the opportunity to describe to you our mechanical processes and the philosophy upon which our business is operating; and I can do so quite lucidly with the assistance of some

---

[3] *Life Insurance Selling*, June 1962.

visual aids in about twenty-two minutes. You can then leisurely determine whether or not you desire to avail yourself of this service. Even if you should decide not to use our facilities, I should very much like to make your acquaintance, and I would like to have you equipped with knowledge of the scope and the character of the work we are doing. I have an appointment in your building at 4:00 on Wednesday afternoon. Could I see you about 4:30 or 4:45 on that day?"

The purpose of Chuck's call is to obtain an appointment, at which time the full scope of his mechanical processes and the philosophy of the operation are described. During the interview he obtains the necessary data to make a complete and comprehensive study of the situation. The first study may reveal a critical need for life and health insurance, or perhaps both.

Chuck is a general agent in Hartford, Connecticut, for the Union Mutual Life Insurance Company. He is a member of the MDRT and of the Membership Committee. Since taking up residence in Hartford in January, 1946, he has devoted much time to community projects and has also served on numerous Boards of Health and Welfare agencies.

TAX APPROACH

Charles Gibbs, one of the top producers of Mutual Benefit of New Jersey, is very successful in getting referrals. Charlie is with the Murrell Brothers in Los Angeles. He writes about thirty life policies each year with 60 per cent repeat sales to clients and 40 per cent referred leads. Charlie introduces himself to his prospect on the telephone, builds prestige by using his referred lead, then says:

"Mr. Williams, I would like to bring to your attention nineteen tax-saving ideas that I have found for businesses. For instance, you can get dollars out of the corporation without income tax . . . legally. You can let your business carry your life insurance for you or pay your family's medical expenses. It will take three minutes for me to show these nineteen tax-saving ideas to you. Then I can determine which will be of value to you. Would the morning or the afternoon be more convenient for you?" [4]

---

[4] *The Insurance Field,* January 20, 1961.

When the appointment has been granted, Charlie follows through on the three-minute time, which is the time allotted to *show* the nineteen tax-saving ideas to the prospect. Charlie walks into the prospect's office with his watch in his hand, pulls out a card listing the nineteen tax-saving ideas and gives a three-minute presentation on them.

I asked Charlie if he left at the end of three minutes. He said, "Yes, unless my watch stops or the prospect asks me to stay."

With nineteen tax-saving ideas, Charlie can uncover a problem that he can help solve with one or more of the ideas.

Charlie concentrates on business insurance for several reasons. There is a larger volume in business insurance. Two or more lives are involved. Businessmen have unlimited needs, and there are many varied uses for business insurance. The prospect doesn't have to die to gain the benefits. In fact, the prospect never dies—his partner dies.

In prospecting for business insurance, Charlie uses his clients (those to whom he has sold personal insurance) and other strong referred leads. He does not attempt to sell business insurance on cold calls. Charlie always telephones for an appointment. He plans his weekly activities on Friday for the following week and makes it a point to have two definite appointments for Monday that have been arranged the preceding week.

DIRECT MAIL

There are many types of letters that may be used as a pre-approach letter to soften a prospect's resistance to the telephone call.[5]

A successful life underwriter in Dallas uses a Christmas letter that is effective, while another life underwriter in New York uses a paycheck letter. Lou W. Schrepel, of American National Insurance Company in Oakland, California, uses a father-son partnership letter that has great appeal to parents, particularly to the father.

[5] *The Insurance Salesman*, December 1961.

Frank Beebe, of Home Life Insurance Company of New York in Los Angeles, uses a Father's Day letter that is extremely effective. Mrs. Dorothy Matzen, of New York Life in Oakland, uses a tax-letter that opens the door to businessmen.

Alan Doud, of the Art Holtzman Agency, Mutual of Omaha, Rochester, New York, makes a telephone call after mailing a letter. Alan's call goes something like this:

1. *Name of prospect.*	1. "Good morning, Mr. Reeves,
2. *Your first and last name.*	2. this is Alan Doud
3. *Name of firm.*	3. with Mutual of Omaha.
4. *Courtesy remark.*	4. How are you this morning?" (Wait for reply.)
5. *Repeat name of prospect.*	5. "Mr. Reeves,
6. *Mention letter.*	6. I sent a letter to you recently. Did you receive it?" (Wait for reply.)
7. *State benefit or idea.*	7. "My purpose in calling is to find out if you have a plan that pays you a regular monthly income when you're sick or hurt and can't work?" (Wait for reply.) "Mutual of Omaha has just such a plan and it pays lifetime benefits for either accident or sickness.
8. *Minimize time.*	8. It will take eighteen minutes to show you how this plan can help you and your family.
9. *Ask for appointment.*	9. Would Tuesday or Wednesday be better for you?"

BUSINESS INSURANCE

R. A. Brown, Jr., of Los Angeles, is a partner with his father, and they specialize in the field of business insurance, deferred compensation plans, and insurance for estate and inheritance taxes. Bob sends a letter to his prospective client and follows with a phone call within seventy-two hours. Bob feels that the letter conditions the prospect's attitude and makes him more receptive to the phone call.

The letter outlines Bob's services, and though the prospect might not remember the details, he does remember the letter. The combination of the letter and the professional call have a tendency to reduce sales resistance during the interview.

Here is Bob's approach to follow-up on a letter:

"Mr. Cook, this is Bob Brown, of R. A. Brown and Son. You recently received a letter from our office that outlined my service and mentioned that I would be calling for an introductory visit to discuss this service with you. Which is the better time for me to see you, the morning or the afternoon?" [6]

Bob's letterhead states that he is in the life insurance business, and the subject of the letter creates interest in the mind of the prospect. The telephone call is effective because of the timing and the fact that Bob is selling an appointment.

Bob does not transact business on the telephone and avoids calls on Monday morning or in the late afternoon. Bob also does not ask for appointments on the hour, because he knows that a busy executive will have appointments at those times.

Bob's principal company is Pacific Mutual Life Insurance Company. Bob is an instructor of Part II, Business Insurance Section of C.L.U. course offered through the University of Southern California. He is also past-president of the Los Angeles C.L.U. Chapter and of the Life Underwriters Association of Los Angeles, Inc.

There is a definite trend toward specialization in most of the professions, including life insurance. Today there are many life underwriters who are specialists in advanced work in pension plans, business insurance, deferred compensation plans, and estate analysis. These specialists are in a position to earn large sums of money, if they prospect on a professional basis.

Many businessmen are aware of some of their problems and will welcome and adopt the solution of insurance when it is brought to their attention. However, time is money to the business-

[6] *The Insurance Salesman*, December 1961.

man. He is more reluctant to see a life underwriter who happens to "drop by" than he is one who makes an appointment at a convenient time.

TAX NEWS LETTER

Ed Mintz has been one of New York Life Insurance Company's leading agents since he joined the firm in 1936, the same year he was admitted to the New York Bar. At the present time, Ed is located in Salinas, California. He has qualified for the MDRT for the sixteenth consecutive year since emerging from the Air Corps in 1946.

During the years when Ed was prospecting for business insurance, he worked out an effective pattern that has proved to be highly successful. These ideas, quite naturally, do not give the entire scope of Ed's program. Ed's program is covered fully in his book, *Selling Business Insurance* (Prentice-Hall, Englewood Cliffs, New Jersey).

Ed sent a tax news letter (the Robert Spindell letter) for many months prior to making a call. He used a combination of direct mail and telephoning for prospects. When he went to Honolulu, he again combined direct mail and the telephone for prospecting. When Ed settled in Salinas, he followed this same procedure.[7]

When Ed calls a potential buyer who has a corporation and is in an estate tax bracket, he says:

> "Mr. Franklin, this is Ed Mintz, of New York Life; there have been some new tax changes to permit your corporation, under certain circumstances, to pay your estate taxes for you at a discount on your death. If you live, there can be income tax savings and a building up of tax-free funds." [8]

This is the opening when Ed sees the prospect to discuss section 303 stock redemptions and qualified profit-sharing trusts. How-

---

[7] *Canadian Insurance*, January 1962.
[8] Reprinted through the courtesy of Prentice-Hall, Englewood Cliffs, N. J.

ever, Ed is prepared in advance to talk about any of the prospect's problems and to offer a concrete suggestion for solution of any problems.

Ed seldom fails to get an appointment on the first call. The personality of a man cannot emerge in a printed approach as it does on the telephone. There is a loss, too, of intonation, inflection, voice quality, empathy, and a dozen other important ingredients that make Ed's call extremely effective.

Ed says that he would never call on anyone without arranging an interview in advance. As Ed stated, "I don't want to see anyone who doesn't want to see me, and I want to see him at an agreed time and place. I spend time in preparation, and I can't afford to spend this time unless I know I'm expected and will have an audience."

Ed's best markets have been with construction and food companies; closed corporation stockholders, particularly where there is already business life insurance; the wives and wealthy members of the family of wealthy deceased, who know by experience the impact of taxes.

The life underwriter who prospects for business insurance knows that if his business work is to have tangible results, he must select his prospects with considerable care. Then he must meet them under favorable circumstances.

PERSONALIZED LETTER

Bob Ralston, of College Life in Indianapolis, uses a personalized letter very effectively. Bob visualizes his prospect as being across the desk when he telephones. Bob's calls are so easy and natural they sound as if he were talking to the prospect across the desk, instead of miles away.

After a sale has been completed, or upon delivery of the policy, whichever is the best time, Bob obtains referrals from his client. Then he makes a smooth transition from the referral to getting a signature on the personalized letter. Within seventy-two hours, he makes a telephone call to the referrals. The logical sequence is similar to that of a referral or a cold call.

1. *Name of prospect.*	1. "Mr. King,
2. *Your first and last name.*	2. . . . this is Bob Ralston
3. *Name of firm.*	3. with College Life.
4. *Courtesy request.*	4. Have you a moment to speak on the phone?" (Wait for reply.)
5. *Repeat name of prospect.*	5. "Mr. King,
6. *Give referral.*	6. you and I haven't met; however, we have a mutual friend in Tom Jones. Tom recently mailed a letter to you telling you of the value of my service. Did you receive it?" (Wait for comment.)
7. *State idea or emphasize benefit.*	7. "I was able to increase the benefits of Tom's insurance without any additional cost to him.
8. *Minimize time.*	8. It will take twenty-two minutes to show you how this was accomplished.
9. *Ask for appointment.*	9. Which would be more convenient for you, the day or the evening?"

A slight variation on the above call might be made in this way:

"Mr. King, this is Bob Ralston. You and I haven't met; however, we have a mutual friend in Tom Jones, who recently sent you a letter regarding my service. Did you receive it?"

SERVICE CALLS

Tom Hinckley, of Equitable Life Assurance Society, Los Angeles, does one of the best jobs of giving excellent service of anyone in the business. Tom is friendly, likes people, and likes to give good service. Out of his good service, he obtains a flow of prospects.

Tom makes it a point to telephone every policyholder one month to six weeks prior to his birthdate or age change. In this way, he can sell additional insurance. He makes another call six months later. These two calls give him a control of service to policyholders. Naturally, he makes additional service calls, on the phone and in personal visits. After a personal visit, Tom will make a few calls similar to this:

"Mrs. Crawford, this is Tom Hinckley, with Equitable Life Assurance. How are you this morning?" (Wait for reply.)

"Mrs. Crawford, Betty Emrick asked me if I would call you. The other evening Betty mentioned that you and your husband had been discussing the type of policy to get for your son's education. I have an idea that will appeal to you and your husband. Will you folks be home Thursday evening, or would Friday be better?"

Joe W. Davis, Volunteer State Life Insurance Company, Chattanooga, Tennessee, gives excellent service to his policyholders, friends, and acquaintances.

Joe's selling ability was evident early in life. At the age of fourteen, he made $36.00 in three lucrative days as a toothpaste salesman.

In 1953, Joe Davis qualified for the MDRT and has qualified each and every year since that time. He is a Life Member of the Cecil Woods Club (President's Top Honor Club) with sixteen years' membership and has won the National Quality Award for the past seventeen years. Joe has served as an instructor of LUTC (Life Underwriter Training Council) and is past-president of the Chattanooga Association of Life Underwriters.

Joe makes service calls to his policyholders, both on the phone and in the field. Joe also makes a service call to potential buyers of life insurance.

"Mr. Freeman, this is Joe Davis, with Volunteer State Life. Have you a moment to speak on the phone?" (Wait for reply.)

"Mr. Freeman, I have no way of knowing whether you may or may not be interested in the purchase of life insurance at this time; however, I have a service that has made it possible for other men in your position to increase their benefits without any additional cost to them. On this basis I should like to meet you and show this service to you. It will take thirty minutes to give you the highlights and for you to determine whether or not my service would be of value to you. Which would be more convenient for you, the first of the week or the latter part?"

Most people believe in purchasing life insurance or living insurance, if the agent makes the right approach. As Will Rogers said, "If you don't believe in life insurance, try dying without it."

Hal L. Nutt, C.L.U., director of Life Insurance Marketing Institute, Purdue University, said, "Disconnect the telephones and large numbers of successful agents would immediately get out of the business."

HOW TO GET
REAL ESTATE APPOINTMENTS
BY TELEPHONE

Discretion of speech is more than eloquence; and to speak agreeably to him with whom we deal is more than to speak in good words, or in good order.

FRANCIS BACON

THE WORK of the real estate salesman covers a broad field of activities, all phases of which are essential to a complete job. He must have a clear understanding of the scope of his responsibilities to insure good service. He must have the ability to talk to people with poise and self-confidence. He must express sincerity, a genuine interest in people, and a sympathetic understanding of their problems. He must convey the idea that he is eager to do the best possible job for them and is trustworthy and reliable. His manner must be businesslike, yet pleasing and cheerful.[1]

SERVICE AT SWITCHBOARD

Service at the switchboard should be given with the objective that it is of the best possible quality. It should be fast, accurate, and outstanding in courtesy and consideration. Features that are of particular importance to persons calling in are prompt answers,

---

[1] Reprinted from *How to Get Appointments by Telephone* by Mona Ling, through the courtesy of Success Motivation Institute, Inc., Waco, Texas.

proper answering phrases, and a friendly, helpful manner at all times. The switchboard operator or secretary should avoid any impression of haste. She should know where the salesmen are, when they will return, and the proper person to handle the calls. Potential buyers do not like to be kicked around from one person to another. They "cool off" if time is wasted in locating some salesman who can give them the information they desire. The switchboard operator or secretary should answer with the name of the firm and with a cheery "Good morning" or "Good afternoon." She should connect the caller with the proper person immediately. Here are some examples of the way telephones may be answered;

"Good morning; Ebby Halliday, Realtors. May we help you?"

"Good afternoon; this is Anne Page. May I help you?"

"Fred W. Jenkins, Realtors; Fred Jenkins speaking."

"Ariel Realtors; this is Marianne Patton. May I help you?"

"Good afternoon; A. R. Langley Company. May we help you?"

THE SALESMAN AND THE TELEPHONE

The salesman should answer his telephone promptly—the first ring, if possible—and identify himself. The tone of voice is extremely important. Your sale begins the moment your telephone rings. If you convey indifference or lack of attention, your caller will maintain that same attitude toward your conversation. If your tone indicates that the caller has interrupted you at a busy time, he will hear it. Transfer your attention immediately to your prospect. Your attention, courtesy, and manner in handling the call will make it possible for you to obtain the necessary information from him so that you can determine his needs. Many times the prospect is reluctant to give his name; however, your voice indicating a desire to be helpful, your diplomatic phrasing, and your tact will give him assurance that you are capable and can be of service to him.

Make the assumption that the caller is ready to buy or he would not have telephoned. Treat him as a prospective buyer, not a conversationalist. Some salesmen do not like to give price over the telephone; other salesmen do discuss price, but avoid talking only about price.

Concentrate on the qualities and features of the house that seem to be uppermost in the prospect's mind. Avoid exaggeration or overstatement. Avoid talking too much. You can listen to the prospect's requirements or needs and still maintain control of the conversation. Review some of the pertinent facts for the prospect. Restate clearly what some of his objectives are and ask diplomatic questions to clarify information. Try to like everyone you talk to during the day and see what happens to your sales.

GET BETTER LISTINGS

Sometime ago I gave my Visual Program on Telephone Technique to over 2,500 realtors at their annual convention of the New Jersey Real Estate Boards at Atlantic City, New Jersey. During the program, I told the audience that "the greatest opportunity to make more money was to get better listings and more salable listings." It has been proved conclusively by successful people that the salesman who can get better listings and more salable listings, at the right price, with owner cooperation, will achieve greater success than the salesman who just gets listings.

Here are a few of the reasons I mentioned, in my program at Atlantic City, as to why some inexperienced salesmen do not get better listings:

1. The salesman doesn't have a reason to seek a listing.

Many salesmen telephone the property owner merely to get a listing without having a good *reason* for telephoning. Establish a "hinge," or plausible reason, whenever possible for asking for the listing and for making the telephone call.

2. The salesman doesn't know why a listing should be given to his firm.

One of the first questions that I ask in training sessions is: "Why should a seller list his property with you and your firm?"

Set the reasons down on paper. Weigh the reasons. Restate them in powerful sales points for your firm.

3. The salesman doesn't have a planned approach.

Many salesmen believe that, if they dial a number and just keep talking, something will happen. They pride themselves on the fact that they can "ad-lib" their way into appointments. Why ad-lib thousands of times during the year and use all of that effort? Why not prepare a planned approach and perfect it? When you ad-lib, you are usually trying to think of what to say, instead of concentrating on the potential buyer or prospective property owner. With a planned approach, you know what you are going to say and can listen to the other person.

4. The salesman doesn't have a good sales story.

The prospect will listen to a good sales story. He will listen if you talk about him, his needs, interests, desires, likes, and dislikes. Ask yourself this question: What does the prospective listing owner want? What does he want to hear? How can your call benefit him? Talk to him with a customer-you attitude and you will gain an attentive listener.

5. The salesman doesn't know how to deliver his approach.

Many salesmen have poor voices, speak too rapidly or slowly. Many do not enunciate clearly or use inflectional variety in their conversation. Nuances of emotion and thought are of great importance to the listener. Read aloud to see how you sound to the prospect. Get another person's opinion on your delivery.

6. The salesman doesn't know how to listen.

Many salesmen talk but don't listen. If the salesman listens to the prospect, he will be able to detect indicators of interest that can be used to his advantage. The salesman should endeavor to learn and perfect a "feedback" mechanism in telephoning.

7. The salesman doesn't know how to ask questions.

In many cases the salesman doesn't know how to ask thought-provoking questions. Nor does he know how to ask qualifying questions. Some salesmen merely ask a few routine questions that merely irritate the prospect.

8. The salesman doesn't know how to overcome objections.

It has been my observation that many calls are ineffective, because the salesman doesn't know how to answer objections. The salesman who knows the answers doesn't worry about objections. The salesman should know how to answer every possible objection that might be given to him during a telephone call or during a personal visit.

9. The salesman doesn't know how to close effectively.

Many salesmen depend on factors other than technique to close interviews or sales. There is a definite technique of closing, which, if used, will pay tremendous rewards.

10. The salesman does not have a professional manner.

Probably more words have been written about this than about any other sales subject within the past few years. It is the accusation that is made most frequently about salesmen. In most cases, this accusation is made because of lack of a professional technique in prospecting or in the initial approach to a prospect.

Dr. G. Herbert True said once, "When you know the prospect knows that you know that you have lost the appointment, then you have lost it."

One of the first lessons that a new real estate salesman or saleswoman should learn is not to waste time on properties that *won't* sell or prospects who *can't* buy. The telephone, if used properly, can save wasted time, motion, energy, and money.

A succesful realtor, Fred W. Jenkins, said, "Talk it out, don't walk it out!"

SOURCES OF LISTINGS

There are many sources of listing properties, a few of which are:

1. Owner's "For Sale" sign or ad.
2. Want ads in newspapers.
3. Natural causes, such as, births, marriages, divorces, deaths, promotions, transfers, retirement, and other causes.
4. Recommendations from satisfied customers.
5. Suggestions from "Centers of Influence."

6. Suggestions from relatives, friends, business or professional acquaintances, firms, banks, etc.
7. Calls, inquiries, timely events, etc.
8. Open houses, home shows, displays.
9. Decline of neighborhood.
10. Personal sales activity.

GETTING LISTINGS

Several years ago, when I was training a group of new real estate salesmen who did not know how to use the telephone I asked one of the men to give a demonstration of getting a listing.

The salesman opened the phone book, selected a number, dialed, and said, "Mrs. Jones, this is Mr. Doe with Brock Realty. Do you by any chance want to sell your home?"

Mrs. Jones answered, "No," and hung up.

I thought this was a very unusual demonstration; however, when I checked with successful and experienced realtors, they assured me that it was not unusual for an untrained and inexperienced salesman to make an abrupt telephone call and ask a direct question: "Do you want to sell your home?"

REAL ESTATE IN ACTION

Fred W. Jenkins, a prominent realtor in Cedar Grove, New Jersey, wrote a forty-five-minute skit, giving examples of the wrong ways to make phone calls and the right ways to make phone calls. This program, *Real Estate in Action,* has been presented to many realty groups, associations, and conventions.

Here is one of Fred's examples from his program of an inexperienced, untrained salesman making a call:

Salesman: "Hello, is this Mrs. Stone?"
Woman: "No, this is Mrs. Johnston."
Salesman: "Oh, I'm sorry. I guess I was mixed up for just a minute. You took so long to answer, I was already looking up your neighbor's number to call next. Say, I've got a real hot buyer here in the office who would like to buy your house. How about a nice quick deal?"

Woman: "Who in the world ever gave you the idea our house is for sale?" (She hangs up.)

Salesman: "Boy, some of these dames are strictly for the birds."

Here is an example of another call from Fred Jenkins' program:

Realtor: "Good morning, Mrs. Young. This is Fred Jenkins, of Fred Jenkins, Realtors, here in the city. Do you have a moment to speak on the phone?"

Mrs. Young: "Yes, I guess so."

Realtor: "Mrs. Young, I wonder if you would do a favor for me?"

Mrs. Young: "Why, yes, if I can. What is it?"

Realtor: "Here is my problem. I am trying to help a very fine young couple, Dr. John Burke and his wife. They have two fine children, seven and nine years of age, and want to find a house in your section to be near Westbrook School. Dr. Burke is employed by Thompson and Thompson in a junior executive capacity, and he's doing some special work in this area. He will be here for at least five years. Dr. Burke has $10,000 in cash to buy a home in your section. Do you by any chance know of anyone who is even so much as thinking that they might want to sell for one reason or another?"

Mrs. Young: "I really don't know. I would have to think about it. I heard there are two houses for sale in the next block, but I think one house was sold. Let me see. You know it's a funny thing, but my husband and I were thinking that we might like to buy a house all on one floor. The doctor has told my husband that it would be better for his health not to climb stairs. But that won't help you right at the moment, because we will want to buy another house before we try to sell this one."

Realtor: "You're wise to find another house first, Mrs. Young. We have a number of attractive all-on-one-floor houses that you would like to know about, I'm sure. I'd like to tell you and your husband about them. Which do you think would be a better time for you, tomorrow morning or the afternoon?"

Mrs. Young: "Oh, the morning would be fine with us. About 11:00 o'clock, if that is all right with you."

Realtor: "Eleven o'clock will be fine with me, Mrs. Young. Thank you very much for your time in talking to me. Good-by."

Mrs. Young: "Good-by."

OUTGOING CALL

Quality should never be sacrificed under any circumstances; however, all of the ingredients of a good call may be incorporated in a very brief conversation.

> Realtor: "Mr. Duncan, this is Fred Jenkins, of Fred Jenkins, Realtors. Do you have a moment to speak to me?"
>
> Duncan: "Yes."
>
> Realtor: "Mr. Duncan, I succeeded in finding a piece of vacant land last night that meets your requirements. I want you to have the first opportunity to see it. Will it be convenient for you to come over this morning, or would you rather make it after lunch?"
>
> Duncan: "After lunch would be better for me. Say about 1:30?"
>
> Realtor: "That's fine with me. I'll be waiting for you. Good-by."
>
> Duncan: "Good-by."

Although this was a brief conversation, several points of good telephone usage were observed.

1. The realtor identified himself and his firm immediately.
2. He was courteous in asking if it was a convenient time for the customer to talk on the phone.
3. He established a purpose for calling immediately.
4. He suggested immediate action and used "which or which."
5. The Realtor waited for the customer to hang the phone up, which was a courtesy.

The realtor should always wait for the customer to replace the receiver of the phone, as the click may be irritating to the customer if the realtor hangs up first. Also, the customer might have a thought, a question, or a request for additional information.

HANDLING INCOMING CALLS

Ebby Halliday, a prominent realtor in Dallas, recently asked this question of a group of realtors. "Why will we spend thousands of dollars in advertising to make the phone ring and so little time in training ourselves and associates on a technique of converting the caller into a prospect?"

Converting a caller into a prospect requires a knowledge of telephone technique and the development of communication skills. It requires your ability to transmit your personality to the person at the other end of the wire, as well as your interest and your desire to be of service.

Ann Carter, realtor, at Chesterton, Indiana, handles incoming calls in this way:

Ann does not answer the phone herself. Her secretary answers, on the first ring, if possible:

"Ann Carter, Real Estate. May I help you?"

Ann keeps a Master Card file next to the phone, and if the person has called before, this card will have all the information on it.

If the person has not called before, information is obtained from the caller, and a Master Card is made.

If the caller wants a great deal of information without making an appointment, Ann sometimes says:

"This is like describing a blue suit over the phone. Try it on. Feel it. Anything I can say won't show you how well it will fit. It's the same with a home. I'll be glad to show it to you. Which would be more convenient for you, the day or the evening?"

AVOID COMPLEX LISTING OR SELLING NEGOTIATIONS

H. Dickey Thacker, president of Earl Thacker Company, Ltd., Honolulu, Hawaii, says his office has about twelve salesmen. They do not have a switchboard system but use a rotary system with four lines and an intercom. They have about ten extensions. A real estate secretary takes the initial calls and passes them to the specific recipient or to the floor person, whichever is applicable. The secretary answers the phone with:

"Earl Thacker Company. May I help you?"

The telephone call is handled courteously, quickly, in a warm friendly tone of voice. The salesmen use the phones primarily for making appointments and try not to give out any complex listing or selling negotiations over the phone.

HANDLING AN INQUIRY

Fred W. Jenkins has demonstrated all types of inquiries in his program, *Real Estate in Action.* These examples are used in his program for realtors.

Phone Rings Once: "Fred Jenkins, Realtor; Fred Jenkins speaking."

Mrs. Reed: "My name is Mrs. Walter Reed, and I would like some information about houses for sale in your area."

Fred: "I'll be glad to give that information to you, Mrs. Reed. Are you looking for a house for yourself or for someone else?"

Mrs. Reed: "Oh, no, we want a house for ourselves."

Fred: "Tell me a little about your family and the type of property you have in mind."

Mrs. Reed: "Well, there are just the two of us, and we thought we'd like something all on one floor."

Fred: "We have a number of fine ranch houses I can tell you about; but first, to save your valuable time, I should like to ask a few more questions. How much do you plan to spend, and have you talked about the amount of cash you would like to invest?"

Mrs. Reed: "We're not too sure about the price, but we have just sold our telephone stock and we have $10,000 for a down payment. You see my husband has been with the telephone company in Moorestown for eighteen years."

Fred: "Thank you for this information, Mrs. Reed. May I ask if you own your home in Moorestown, or if you rent?"

Mrs. Reed: "No, we don't own a home. We've been in an apartment for eight years and have given notice to move the first of February because my husband's business brings him to Atlantic City. In fact, he's staying with the George Blocks, who bought a house through your office last year."

Fred: "Oh, yes, I remember the George Blocks. From what you've told me, Mrs. Reed, I know I can help you and save you and your husband valuable time in running around. If we can sit down together and discuss your requirements more fully, I'm sure we can find what you want. Would tomorrow morning or the afternoon be better for you and your husband?"

Mrs. Reed: "I think the morning would be all right, say about 10:00 o'clock. I'll call my husband to see if that time would be all right with him and will call you back."

Fred: "Thank you, Mrs. Reed. You most probably would prefer to come to my office, where we can have complete privacy in our discussion. I will give the address to you when you call back and will direct you, if your husband needs any help in locating my office. I'll wait here until you call."

Mrs. Reed: "I'll only be a few moments. Good-by."

Fred: "Good-by, Mrs. Reed."

INQUIRY ABOUT AN ADVERTISEMENT

Phone Rings Once: "Fred Jenkins, Realtor; Fred Jenkins speaking."

Mr. Carter: "This is Cliff Carter. I wonder if you'd be good enough to give me a little information about the house you advertised in last night's paper for $16,500?"

Fred: "Why, certainly, Mr. Carter, I'll be glad to. It's a well-designed colonial, in excellent condition, situated in the Bradley district. Where do you live, Mr. Carter?"

Mr. Carter: "We live on Moon Drive. We've been here about a year and are not too familiar with the city."

Fred: "In that case you would like to have a copy of our city map. It shows all the sections of town, the schools, public buildings, golf courses, transportation facilities, as well as many other important locations. I'll be glad to send you a copy. C-A-R-T-E-R. Is that correct?"

Mr. Carter: "Yes. The street number is 2906 Moon Drive."

Fred: "Thank you, Mr. Carter. If you will tell me your particular needs, I will do my best to help you. It will help me to know the type of house you now live in, and what you like and don't like about it."

Mr. Carter: "Well, we now have a four-room apartment, on which we've given notice to move in sixty days, and we want to get into a six- or seven-room colonial."

Fred: "We have a fine selection of houses this size. Would you mind telling me if you plan to pay cash for a house, or would you want a mortgage?"

Mr. Carter: "Thanks for the compliment, but $5,000 in cash is what we hoped to buy a house with."

Fred: "That's fine, Mr. Carter. We should have no trouble in arranging everything so as to make your change of address a real pleasure. You will want to start the ball rolling as soon as possible, won't you?"

Mr. Carter: "Yes, we'd like to get started right away on making the change."

Fred: "In that case, you and Mrs. Carter should arrange to come to the office so we can determine what your needs are and discuss some of our choice houses. Which would be better, this afternoon or this evening?"

Mr. Carter: "I guess this evening would be better. How about 8:00 o'clock?"

Fred: "Eight o'clock would be fine with me. Thank you very much for your information. I'll see you here in my office at 8. Good-by, Mr. Carter."

Mr. Carter: "Good-by." (Hangs up first.)

BATTLE OF "GETTING THE NAME"

A demonstration of an inexperienced, untrained salesman from *Real Estate in Action* was given to illustrate the *wrong* way to attempt to get the name of a person who made an inquiry.

Salesman: "Hello."

Prospect: "Hello, is this Harris and Brown, Realtors?"

Salesman: "Yes, who's this?"

Prospect: "All I want to know is, where is the house located that you advertised in the news?"

Salesman: "What's your name?"

Prospect: "I just want to see the outside of the house first."

Salesman: "I have to have your name first."

Prospect: "Do you have to have that?"

Salesman: "Yes, I do before I can give you any information."

Prospect: "Why?"

Salesman: "Because it's company policy."

Prospect: "All I want to know is where the house is located first."

Salesman: "I can't tell you until I get your name."

Prospect: "Forget it." (Click of receiver.)

THE BUYER WHO WON'T GIVE HIS NAME

Frequently a buyer withholds his name when asking for information because he doesn't want to be "sold," or perhaps he just wants to add to his store of knowledge before he becomes serious about buying. There are other reasons, too, sometimes involving ulterior motives.

Fred Jenkins says, "The real estate salesman may lose a profitable sale, if he assumes that the buyer is not worthwhile because he appears secretive. This type of buyer should be a challenge to the salesman's sales skill. Now is the time to be prepared to *sell* the inquirer on the advantages of giving his name. Be prepared to offer something the buyer might want."

Fred gives these suggestions for getting the name of the caller:

1. Give extraordinary service.
2. Give a map of your area.
3. Give a brochure of your area.
4. Give picture brochures of listed properties.
5. Give descriptions of a number of competitive properties in buyer's price class.
6. Give instruction concerning mortgage financing available.
7. Give special services that you or your office can offer the buyer. (These special services are available only if you have the person's name and address for mailing, of if there can be a face-to-face meeting.)

RELUCTANCE TO GIVE NAME

The following procedures are used by Fred and his associates.

Phone Rings Once: "Fred Jenkins, Realtor; Fred Jenkins speaking."

Caller: "Mr. Jenkins, I wonder if you would tell me the location of the $19,000 split you have advertised?"

Fred: "I'll be glad to, Mrs. —— May I have your name please?"

Caller: "Well, all I really wanted to do was drive by."

Fred: "I can appreciate that you would want to see the house. Exterior appearances are important; however, I'll be more than glad to be your chauffeur. But before I do that, I may be able to save you a lot of time. Tell me, how many children do you have?"

Caller: "We have two children. A boy, eleven, and a girl, nine."

Fred proceeds with qualifying questions regarding the family, their needs, wants, desires. After a few questions, the name is given automatically, without any reluctance from the prospect.

GIVE COMPETITIVE PROPERTIES
IN BUYER'S PRICE CLASS

Caller: "May I have the address to that $19,000 split you have advertised?"

Salesman: "Why, yes, I'll be glad to give that information to you. Would you excuse me while I get the listing card? It has the taxes, the size of the lot, and all of the information." (Pause briefly.) "Or, better still, may I say this: before I wrote that ad I lined up three comparable houses; but before I tell you about all of these houses, tell me how many children do you have?"

Proceed with qualifying information. Fred Jenkins uses a list of qualifying questions, similar to those listed on page 120.

CALLER WANTS A RENTAL

Here is a familiar call that every office gets with a fair degree of regularity. Mrs. Jones wants a rental. She looks in the telephone directory or in a newspaper, selects a firm and dials the number. If the untrained salesman happens to answer the telephone, the conversation might go something like this:

Caller: "Do you have any five- or six-room houses for rent?"

S/man: "Don't make me laugh. We haven't seen a rental in a year. You ought to buy something."

Caller: "That's impossible. You see we don't have any money." (Click of receiver.)

If Mrs. Jones is fortunate enough to have the experienced salesman answer her call, the conversation would be completely different. An example from *Real Estate in Action* is given.

Caller: This is Mrs. Jones. Do you have any five- or six-room houses for rent?"

Fred: "I wish we did, Mrs. Jones, but perhaps I can help you anyway. How much rent do you feel you can pay?"

Caller: "We don't want to pay over $150."

Fred: "Would you tell me something about your family, Mrs. Jones? How many children do you have?"

FAMILY

————————Boys————————Girls

————————Man————————Wife

Others————————————————

MUST HAVE

————————BR————————Bath

————————DR————————Extra

————————Gar————————Age

Miscl.————————————————

Col.————Eng.————Split————Bung————

Other————————Lot————————

————————————————————

Called Re:————————————————

Name————————————————

Address————————————————

Comments:————————————————

AT PRESENT

Own————————Rent————————

No hurry————————House sold————————

Must move by:————————————

PRICE RANGE

$————————To $————————

Cash down $————————————

Monthly pay. $————————————

Trans.————Bus————Train————

New York————————————————

Newark————————————————

School————————————————

Price————————

Phone————————

Date————————

Caller: "We have two children, Billy and Susan. Susan is the older and will start school in September."

Fred: "Here is an idea, Mrs. Jones. We have a three-bedroom colonial, not too far from the Wildwood Grade School. It is an excellent school, as you probably know. After a down payment, you can carry it for about $110 a month, which is $40 to $50 a month less than it would be if it were rented."

Caller: "That sounds wonderful, but we don't have very much money. We only have $5,000 saved at this time."

Fred: "Mrs. Jones, I feel quite certain that I can be of help to you and your family. Would you and your husband like to come over to my office this afternoon or this evening to discuss how I can be of help to you?"

Caller: "We can come this evening, Mr. Jenkins. Would 8 o'clock be all right?"

Fred: "Eight o'clock would be fine. My office is about ten minutes from the Traymore Hotel. I'll be looking forward to seeing you at 8."

Caller: "All right. Good-by."

Fred: "Good-by, Mrs. Jones."

Fred and his associates convert renters into buyers by giving helpful information and by giving extraordinary service.

Ebby Halliday, in Dallas, Texas, says that she and her associates convert about 80 per cent of the inquirers for rentals into buyers of properties.

DO'S AND DON'T'S OF TELEPHONE CALLING

From keeping one ear to the telephone, listening to conversation in her office, Ebby Halliday has been able to analyze their failures and successes in the use of the telephone. Here are some of the suggestions that have helped her and her associates do a better job on the telephone.

1. Have a pleasant, sincere, positive voice.
2. Smile when you talk on the telephone.
3. Don't have a shabby word-wardrobe. Use descriptive words to create a mental image.
4. Synchronize your rate of speech with the rate of speech of the person to whom you are speaking.

5. When calling a client, ask if it is convenient to talk.
6. Make your conversations short, lucid, and meaningful.
7. Never keep someone "holding" while you speak to someone else. You should have had the information before you in the first place. If an emergency does arise with another call, ask if you may call him back. He may be busy, too.
8. Never have your secretary place a call if you aren't ready to talk. It's all right if it's the other way around.
9. Don't do all of the talking. Give the person on the other end of the line an opportunity to answer you, to ask questions, or to make comments. Never interrupt!
10. Be as courteous voice-to-voice as you are in a personal visit.

USE OF YOUR NAME

Ever since Will Shakespeare made his well-known remark, "What's in a name? That which we call a rose by any other name would smell as sweet." (*Romeo and Juliet*), people have tried to come up with the answer.

If you ask Jesse James, "What's in a name?" he will tell you, "Sales." Jesse James is one of General Development Corporation's top salesmen in Florida. Jesse earns more in a year selling homes than the notorious badman ever got in all of his years as the Old West's No. 1 bank robber.

"Jesse James is a wonderful name for my real estate sales," says Jesse. "People never forget me. Sometimes potential customers come down to Florida to look over a lot or a house. Then they return North. Later, they may come back to purchase. If they do, they always remember they once met Jesse James."

Every real estate salesman doesn't have a name as easy to remember or as hard to forget as "Jesse James." However, every salesman can repeat his name slowly with a slight pause, so the prospect can hear it. If the salesman has an unusual name, he can make some remark about his name that will give the prospect a mental image of it.

"Mr. Jones, (slight pause) this is Walter Chamberlain."

INTER-CITY REAL ESTATE REFERRAL SERVICE

The telephone can help the salesman establish a fine salesman-client relationship, in one city or in several cities. For example, several hundred brokers located in key cities throughout the country maintain an excellent broker-client relationship.

Ralph W. Pritchard, vice-president of Joseph A. Thorsen Company, La Grange, Illinois, says: "The phone is a basic tool for us, and while I am not always sure it is used properly, it certainly does wonderful things.

"As a typical example, we have an organization called the Inter-City Real Estate Referral Service. This is a group of several hundred brokers located in key cities throughout the country. Our alliance is to provide each other with referrals of customers who are living in our area and going to theirs.

"We are one of the leading concerns in this matter, and we have a section of our organization that uses the telephone as the means of communication with the client here. The story of Inter-City is explained to the client and permission obtained to refer them to our cooperative broker in the city to which they are moving. We then call the broker in the receiving city immediately. He makes another call directly to the client in our town and sets up whatever appointments are necessary or gives out information that will be helpful."

TELEPHONE AIDS EXPANSION

General Development Corporation advertises that it is the nation's first builder of complete cities. It owns or controls nearly 200,000 acres of Florida's finest coastal land and has total assets of nearly $200 million. General Development's operations embrace every phase of community building: the acquisition, planning, and engineering of the land; the construction of roads and bridges; the erection of commercial and recreational structures; the building of homes; the planning and construction of utilities—everything from raw land to completed community.

An idea of the scope of the operation, planning, and work of General Development might be gathered from one community. Five years ago, Port Charlotte, 92,700 acres, midway between Sarasota and Fort Myers, was undeveloped land. Some 110,000 homesites have been sold there, and nearly 4,000 homes have been sold, built, and occupied, with current construction at the record rate of ten a day. The community has three shopping centers, two water and sewer systems, more than 250 miles of paved roads, nearly 100 miles of water frontage; parks, school sites, nine churches, a championship golf course, two public beaches, a fishing pier, yacht club and marina, several recreational centers— one with an Olympic-size pool. The total population is 10,000, with an estimate of a population approaching one million, making this community one of Florida's major cities.

Port Charlotte is one of eight preplanned communities with similar activities—Port St. Lucie, Port Malabar, Port St. John, Sebastian Highlands, Vero Beach Highlands, Vero Shores, and Pompano Beach Highlands.

The sales of General Development Corporation were $68,400,- 752 in 1961. In a statement regarding the anticipated sales of General Development, H. A. Yoars, president, had this to say: "I expect General Development to report sales of somewhere around $80 million in 1962."

In personal interviews with several executives and top salesmen of General Development Corporation, each person stressed the fact that the telephone had played an important part in the development of the company and its successful sales record.

SELLING APPOINTMENTS

"The telephone is a marvelous business-getter," said Barbara Lamont, of General Development's Miami Beach office.

Barbara has a simple approach. She prefers to ask a question at the beginning of the telephone conversation. She has an answer for "no" and an answer for "yes."

"Good morning, Mr. Smith. This is Barbara Lamont, with the

General Development Corporation. Have you heard of our organization?"

Mr. Smith either says "no" or "yes." If his answer is "no," then Barbara gives him a brief outline of General Development's operations. If his answer is "yes," then she invites him to visit the Cape Canaveral area with the purpose of getting him interested in an investment.

> "Mr. Smith, I would like to acquaint you with an excellent investment opportunity in the Cape Canaveral area, which, as you know, is now the spotlight of the world. We are building a beautiful city at Port Malabar. It will take twenty-two minutes to go over this investment idea with you and for you to determine whether or not it might be of interest to you. Which would be more convenient for you to hear about this investment, the day or the evening?"

Irwin Lieberman, of the Miami Beach office, prospects among businessmen for the most part. Irwin knows many people in the Miami Beach area and has a tremendous source of prospects for investments. Irwin invites the prospect to take a trip to the homesite to see the investment before he closes the sale.

> "Mr. Jones, this is Irwin Lieberman, of General Development Corporation. My purpose in calling is to invite you to take a trip with us to Port St. Lucie. There is no obligation or cost. I want you to see the unusual investment opportunities at Port St. Lucie. If you like these investment opportunities, may I ask how much you would like to start with as a down payment?"

Ed Katz says, "Don't give curbstone information. The salesman makes the mistake frequently of trying to give too much information over the telephone."

Ed prefers to telephone at home. He believes this gives him a relaxed feeling that will be transmitted to the prospect. Ed believes that the salesman should not transmit hurry, impatience, or high pressure to the prospect.

Ed frequently talks to people to get referrals, who might be interested in a good investment. Then he says, "You might be interested in this investment for yourself." In many cases, the person has become interested in hearing about the investment and listens to Ed's story. He then tells the story of rapid growth of Port Charlotte, Port St. Lucie, and Port Malabar, without any haste in getting the story told. He is sincere, which can be detected by the listener; he answers all questions that are asked of him without being evasive; he offers extraordinary service to all.

Mrs. Rose Spievack says, "I play most of my selling by ear. If I can make my presentation short and to the point, I do. But if other methods are indicated, I go along with the customer. My sales presentation depends on the client. I listen for cues."

Rose also works in the Lowry Clark office at Miami Beach. As Lowry has been tremendously interested in telephone techniques for many years, his associates are also interested in the effective use of the telephone.

Rose opens her conversation with:

> "Good evening, Mr. Brown. This is Rose Spievack, with General Development Corporation. Have you a moment to speak on the phone?" (Reply, "Yes.")
>
> "My purpose in calling is to request the courtesy of twelve minutes of your time to give you a few highlights of a sound and profitable investment. Are you interested in an investment?" (Reply, "Yes.")
>
> "Mr. Brown, it will take twelve minutes for me to show this investment idea to you and for you to determine whether or not it would be a good investment for you. Would this afternoon or this evening be better for you?"

In order to save both her time and her prospect's, Rose frequently asks a qualifying question: "If I can show you how you can make money, are you in the position to pay $10 down?"

SPEED AND ACCURACY IN COMMUNICATIONS

"Speed and accuracy are highly important factors in the operation of our far-flung sales organization," said E. B. Richardson. "These are provided in full measure by our communications network, with an appreciable savings in time and money for all concerned."

General Development utilizes the 83B2 Teletypewriter Selective Calling System, designed and engineered by the Long Lines Department of the American Telephone and Telegraph Company. This system provides a continuous bridge of communications between member offices and the up-to-the-minute company information center.

With its twenty-five-station network in operation a full sixteen hours a day most days in the week, General Development is one of the largest single users in its field of this modern means of communication. Some idea of the scope of General Development's operations may be gathered from the fact that more than 280,000 words a month are flashed over 3,500 miles of leased wires that now feed into the Miami headquarters from sales outlets in thirteen states, the District of Columbia, and twenty-one cities.

Their efficient communications system is an invaluable aid in the sale of both homes and homesites. The many details involved in a home sale are greatly facilitated by this two-way system. It also speeds the closing of lot sales, as it provides immediate information on the availability of sites and eliminates the possibility of duplicate sales.

In addition to the vast communications system in the United States, General Development has to keep close contact with its overseas operation, which now has three sales outlets in the Pacific area, fourteen in Latin America, one in Asia, sixteen in Europe, and one each in North Africa, Japan, and Okinawa.

General Development has also extended its roster of franchised agents to Lahore, West Pakistan, and Rabat, Morocco. It has sales representatives in Paris, France; Madrid, Spain; Antwerp, Belgium; Livorno, Italy; London, England; Ankara, Turkey.

TELEPHONE IS A BRIDGE OF COMMUNICATIONS

"The telephone," says General Development President H. A. Yoars, "has played an all-important part in our becoming the world's largest community building organization.

"In the daily operation of our business, the telephone and our high-speed private wire teletype network give special meaning to the familiar business axiom 'time is money.'

"With some 300 sales offices across the nation, in Canada, Latin America, Europe, and the Pacific area, the success of our operation depends largely upon the speed and accuracy provided by these communications media.

"Our headquarter's switchboard handles hundreds of calls daily, some from as far away as Tokyo or Lahore, Pakistan, while more than 280,000 words a month are flashed over our teletype network.

"In addition to providing a continuous bridge of communications between member offices, our teletype network also provides an up-to-the-minute company information service.

"It is an invaluable aid in the sale of both homes and homesites. The many details involved in a home sale are greatly facilitated by this two-way system."

The teletype is a bridge of communications, connecting 97.6 of the telephones in the world.

TELEPHONE QUIZ ON LISTINGS

Ask yourself the following questions to determine your strong and weak points. Assign a value of ten points to each *yes* answer. Those questions that you answer *no* will show your weak points.

	YES	NO
1. Do you know about every listing you have?	——	——
2. Do you keep a list of newspaper ads and listings ready for quick reference?	——	——
3. Do you devote a certain amount of time each week to telephoning buyers of past years to see how their purchase is serving them?	——	——
4. Do you spend time in establishing good relationships with past buyers and in obtaining new listings from them?	——	——
5. Do you devote a certain amount of time each week to telephoning "centers of influence"?	——	——
6. Do you thank relatives, friends, clients, and "centers of influence" for information or suggestions or customers?	——	——
7. Do you sell your name to prospects so they will remember you on call-backs?	——	——
8. Do you keep your word in calling prospects back?	——	——
9. Do you instill prospects with confidence that your service will be of value to them?		
10. Do you follow a consistent method of prospecting?	——	——

HOW TO OVERCOME
OBJECTIONS

A human being can go without food longer than he can go without human dignity.

HARRY GOLDEN

SOME TIME AGO, J. A. Livingston related some interesting sales experiences in his column, *"The Business Outlook,"* which appeared in the *Detroit News* and other newspapers.[1]

BUYER ASKS A QUESTION

I am indebted for this to Robert W. Brost, Philadelphia zone manager of American Motors Corporation, and formerly in the New York zone. A man dropped into a New York Buick showroom, looked over the display, pointed to a particular car, and asked the salesman:

"How much is that?"

"What kind of car are you driving?" the salesman asked.

"Perhaps you didn't understand my question," the customer replied. "I asked the price of that car. It looks like what I want."

"I heard you, but I'd like to know what year car you're driving, so I'll know what I can offer you in trade."

"Look," said the customer, "maybe I don't have a car. My

---

[1] Reprinted through courtesy of J. A. Livingston, syndicated column, "The Business Outlook," in *Detroit News*, May 21, 1961.

car doesn't enter into this. Maybe I'm not going to turn in a car. I want to know what that car's worth."

"I know," the salesman sputtered, "but I have to know what the trade is—what you're turning in, or whether it's for cash."

Disgusted, the man walked out and went to another Buick dealer. As Brost tells it, he got the same kind of "oogy-talk." Then he tried a Ford dealer. Ditto. Finally, he went to a Rambler dealer. If you think he received a straight answer—"The price tag's on the windshield; exactly $2,322.42 as equipped"—read on.

The customer got exactly the same "wrap-around word-shield" as at Buick and Ford. That's how Brost got into the act.

Though the man was not hep to automobile trade "fancy-pancy," he was a torrid man with a letterhead and typewriter. Off went a letter to George Romney, American Motors president. The writer said he'd read of Romney as a straight shooter, he'd heard of American Motors as a company trying to give the customer a square deal, but what kind of salesmanship was this?

When you ask the price, the salesman answers, "What kind of car you got?" The last time he went to Tiffany's to buy his wife a wrist watch, the writer pointed out, the salesman didn't ask, "What make watch is she wearing?"

Romney forwarded the letter to Brost with a notation, "Do something about this?" A Rambler dealer made the sale—through sheer dint of customer boiling point. Brost draws a moral: salesmanship isn't what is used to be.

Many agree that the art of salesmanship is more preached than practiced. A well-to-do couple recently went to a large department store to buy a couch. They inspected furniture with a salesman. Finally the husband said, pointing to two couches:

"I like the big arms on that and the sloping back on that. Do you have something that combines both features?"

The salesman: "Are you trying to be difficult?"

The customer: "Look, you're selling me, I'm not selling you." He took his wife's arm and walked out.

As J. A. Livingston sums it up: "That wasn't salesmanship; that was murder!"

THE "FEARFUL" FIVE

Donn Mason, author of the recording *How to Overcome Sales Objections*, says: "By putting your actual objections, as you hear them, under a microscope you will find that you encounter a maximum of *five basic objections*. What confuses you and gives the impression that there are scores of objections is that the five basic ones can be worded in hundreds of ways." [2]

Here are the five basic objections, as given by Donn Mason:

1. Doesn't meet requirements.
2. Competition.
3. Lack of finance.
4. Consult with associate.
5. Previous trouble unadjusted.

Now the breakdown as to some of the ways these objections are voiced to you:

Doesn't meet requirements

Price is too high; quality too low; slow turnover; construction or design not right; materials or ingredients don't meet specs; packaging not satisfactory; freight not prepaid; profit margin too small; no cooperative advertising; delivery too slow; not enough variety; shipping point too far away; no displays supplied.

Competition

Satisfied with present supplier; too many lines now; present supplier knows our needs; our customers ask for Widget; our salesmen will only sell our present line; we have a complete stock of Widget; Widget has a better selection; your service isn't as good as Widget's.

Lack of finance

Can't afford it now; over-supplied now; must sell what we have; too much of an investment; no money; must use present stock first.

2 Donn Mason, *How to Overcome Sales Objections*. Reprinted through the courtesy of Success Motivation Institute, Inc., Waco, Texas.

Consult with associate

I'll talk it over with the engineer; my partner must OK it, too; I'll discuss it with our salesmen and distributors; must have the merchandise manager's approval; the final decision rests with the owner; it's up to the plant superintendent; the board must decide.

Previous trouble unadjusted

Your company didn't treat us right years ago; the salesman before you gave us a raw deal; you change salesmen too often; too many difficulties with past shipments; have had trouble with your service; you back-order too much.

Donn says, "A smooth, sound procedure for *avoiding an argument*, and still overcoming an objection, is to 'Turn the objection into a question.' If done skillfully, it's most effective. I call this technique a 'persuasive objection-handler.'"

Buyer: "Sorry, but your price is too high. The product we use is 10 per cent cheaper than yours."

Salesman: "Then what you are wondering is, 'Why pay a 10 per cent premium for a similar product?' Is that the question, Mr. Buyer?"

Donn Mason is giving the "whys" and "wherefores" of overcoming objections in the field; however, these same techniques may be developed in overcoming objections on the telephone.

The same objections, or similar objections, will be given to the salesman on the telephone that would be given to him in the sales interview. As most successful salesmen will agree, the best thing that can happen to a salesman is to receive objections. When a prospect objects, he is buying.

OBJECTIONS ARE OPPORTUNITIES TO CLOSE

Objections are "opportunities to close" the appointment on the phone or the sale in the interview. When a prospect gives an objection, he is asking for additional information or for clarification or information. If the salesman will assume that every objection is an opportunity to close, he will answer the question or give the information with effective closing techniques. However, if the salesman just tries to answer a question or give additional information without attempting to close the appointment or the sale, he weakens his presentation and reduces his chances of closing.

When you have an opportunity to close, use this simple technique:

    A. Build ego—with a deference transition or ego-building statement.
    B. Switch—from the objection to an advantage of the plan, idea, or benefit.
    C. Minimize time—ask for a brief interview to acquaint the prospect with this plan, idea, product.
    D. Ask for appointment—get action into the presentation.

For example, the prospect might tell John Doe, of the Doe Business Services, that he is busy. John Doe's answer might be: (A) "Mr. Smith, I can appreciate the fact that you are busy; that's why I telephoned. (B) However, Mr. Executive of the XYZ Company, said this service had saved their company both time and money. (C) The purpose of my call is to request the courtesy of twenty-two minutes of your time to show this service to you. (D) Which would be more convenient for you, the morning or the afternoon?"

If it is not necessary to minimize time or to request a specific amount of time, omit step "C".

Here are some typical objections given to automotive salesmen in response to telephone calls about buying a new car. The answers given are printed through the courtesy of the Ford Motor Company, Detroit, Michigan.

OBJECTIONS TO BUYING A CAR

"They're not economical, like foreign cars."

    "It is true, Mr. Smith, that some smaller cars have better gas milage, but the Falcon has many counteracting benefits. Parts and service are inexpensive and available everywhere, and the Falcon is a full size, six-passenger car on the inside. But I'd rather show you these advantages, so you can see them for yourself. I can bring a new Falcon to your home tonight at 7:00 or 7:30. Which would be the best time for you?"

"I don't want a scaled-down big car."

"I'm glad you brought that up, Mr. Jones. You'll like a Falcon, because every part of this car is entirely new and made just for it. That includes a special economy six-cylinder engine. You would have to see the Falcon features in person to appreciate them. Would you like to take a demonstration ride in one tonight? I could have a new Falcon at your home by 7:30. Would that be soon enough?"

"Foreign cars are made better."

"It's certainly true, Mr. White, that other countries have contributed many worthwhile engineering features; but if you were to examine a Falcon yourself, you'd be amazed at the many unusual features. The Falcon doesn't take a back seat to any car at or near its price on quality and features. You'll be able to tell that, I'm sure, as soon as you see it. I can have a Falcon over at your home at 6:00 this evening. Would that time be all right, or would 7:00 be better for you?"

"I've heard the gas mileage isn't so hot."

"I'm glad you brought that up, Mr. Black. I've heard that, too, about some of the new compact cars. But the Falcon really does deliver up to thirty miles per gallon. Ford proved Falcon's economy with the Experience Run, U.S.A. in a 220,000-mile driving test over all kinds of terrain. I'd like to show you the actual figures along with a new Falcon. Which would be better for you, the earlier part of the evening, around 6:30, or the latter part, around 8:30?"

"They cost too much."

"A car is an important purchase; however, the Falcon is a full-size car on the inside—a full-time car that can take six people anywhere. That's why it costs more than some of the four-passenger imported cars. You have a (name and year of prospect's car) don't you? (Get answer.) With that in trade, you'll find a new Falcon will cost you much less than you might think. I can bring a new Falcon over to your plant this afternoon. Which would be better for you, the earlier part of the afternoon, around 1:30 or the latter part, around 4:00?"

REAL ESTATE OBJECTIONS

Fred Jenkins says that when you call the prospect, you have interrupted him and he wants to get back to what he was doing. Therefore, you have to make your idea attractive to the prospect.

"I'd like to think it over."

"Mr. Smith, I can understand why you would want to think it over. Selling your home is an important undertaking, requiring careful planning. One thing that will help you is to know what other houses like yours have sold for. We have exact information regarding such sales that I will be glad to bring over to show you and Mrs. Smith tonight. What time would be better for you—7:00 or 7:30?"

"I'm not ready to sell; but when I do, I plan to give the listing to Donald North."

"You certainly won't make any mistake by giving the house to Donald North. They have a fine office. We've had a great many cooperative sales with them. Are you giving them the listing this week?" (Reply—"No.")

"Mr. Jones, did you know that you are more likely to get a better price for your *house* if it is sold within thirty days?" (Wait for answer.) "We have a very interesting chart showing the actual results of recent sales. This is information that can help you to sell your house. It will take twenty-two minutes to show this information to you. What time this evening would be better for you—7:00 or 8:00?"

"We don't want any brokers."

"Mr. Black, when men tell me they don't need our service, I find it is usually for one of two reasons—either they feel they can save the commission, or they have had poor experience with a previous broker. Would you mind telling me which of these is true in your particular case?"

"Can't you tell me over the phone?"

"Mr. White, the merchandising plan for selling your house is far too important for me to describe in a few moments over the phone. It will take thirty minutes to illustrate it for you in person. Which will be better for me to do this, the day or the evening?"

"We don't want a lot of brokers tramping through our house."

"Mr. Brown, I can appreciate how you feel. I wouldn't want that either if I were in your position. However, we make a detailed profile of your house and arrange for a professional picture to be taken, so that better informed brokers and salesmen will not need to make needless trips through your house. Does that sound like a satisfactory arrangement to you?"

DIRECT SALES OBJECTIONS

"I can't afford one now."

"That's perfectly all right, Mrs. Jones. The purpose of my call is to request the courtesy of twenty-two minutes to demonstrate our appliance. Then when you are ready to make a purchase, you will know about our brand and its superior quality over other brands. Would the morning or the afternoon be better for you?"

"Your product is higher-priced than other similar products."

"I'm glad you brought that up, Mrs. Smith, and you will be interested to know about the superior quality of our product over other similar products. However, it would save your valuable time if I could show you these advantages in your home. Which would be a better time for me to show our product to you, the morning or the afternoon?"

"Can't you tell me over the phone?"

"I'd be glad to, Mr. Black; however it would save your valuable time to see a colored film that my company has produced about our product. This film tells a complete story about our product and answers any questions that you might have. It takes fifteen minutes to show this film to you. Which would be more convenient for you, the day or the evening?"

"You will just be wasting your time."

"Mr. White, I'll be glad to gamble a few minutes of my time against your open-mindedness about a new home improvement that will save many dollars for you over the next few years. You are interested in saving money on home improvements, aren't you?"

"Your rates are too high."

"I'd probably feel the same way that you do if I were in your position, Mr. Jones; however, it will take ten minutes for me to show you how we can put extra dollars in your pocket without any financial strain on you whatsoever. Would the day or the evening be more convenient for you?"

"I can't do anything right now."

"I'd be the last person in the world, Mr. Johnson, to ask you to do something that you didn't want to do. But tell me, would this saving be of benefit to you and your family over the next few years?"

DIFFICULTY IN OVERCOMING OBJECTIONS

In a recent article for the *Life Association News,* Washington, D.C., I wrote about the techniques of overcoming objections for life underwriters. Through the courtesy of Sam P. Gaglio, editor, part of this article is being reprinted.[3]

Ben Rocca, Jr., told me that early in his career he had great difficulty in overcoming objections. He would get inside the door of a potential buyer eager to give his sales talk. The prospect would ask, "Are you selling insurance?"

Ben used to answer, "Yes."

In many cases the interview was terminated at that point. As the interviews went by, Ben discovered that few prospects wanted to "buy insurance." As the years went by, Ben gained experience in talking to people in terms they could understand. He found another method of answering this objection. To this same question, he would answer:

"No. That is not right. Our organization helps you to plan—
(1) For your death.
(2) For your wife's death.
(3) For your total disability.
(4) For "You," just living.
(5) For your retirement."

This answer get better results and a more pleasing reaction. Somehow the prospect seemed to understand and to accept this answer.

As Ben gained more insight into human nature, he learned, too, why the prospect objects. He learned that the prospect has certain basic "buyer" fears. When the prospect is confronted with a

---

[3] Reprinted through the courtesy of *Life Association News,* 1962.

buying situation, he stalls, makes excuses, offers resistance and objections. The "buyer" fears are present at the point of the telephone in requesting an appointment, or in a sales interview requesting signature on an application or an order blank. As objections, for the most part, come from these fears, they are natural and normal.

During an all-day Sales Workshop on Telephone Technique for the St. Louis Life Underwriters Association, I covered this point with many illustrations on colored slides to substantiate my statements. Several life underwriters commented about this subject later. One agent said he had never considered the possibility of objections being anything but unnatural. This approach gave him hope that he could overcome his fear of objections in both prospecting and selling. He later wrote to say that he was comfortable in telephoning or selling and had gained facility and skill in overcoming objections.

BUYER FEARS

Objections are natural and normal. Every prospective buyer has certain basic "buyer" fears when he is confronted with a buying situation. These three basic buying fears are:

1. Will I make a mistake if I buy?
2. Will my benefits equal the price I pay?
3. What will others think about my purchase?

These same basic buying fears are aroused when a salesman requests an interview, because most people believe their independence of judgment will be jeopardized by the salesman's clever arguments, experience, and persuasive skills in a selling interview.

It is perfectly natural for the prospect to object to the appointment or to the sale. If the prospect did not object, there would be no demand for outside salesmen. The potential buyers would buy what they wanted "over a counter." People have to be persuaded, convinced, and motivated to give you an appointment or to sign an application.

It has been my experience in training that the salesman who recognizes "buyer" fears and learns how to face them on a mature level develops greater facility and skill in overcoming objections. The belief that objections are unnatural and that the prospects are difficult, negative, and stubborn, tends to destroy creativity in the development of skills and techniques in telephoning and in the sales interview.

KINDS OF OBJECTIONS

There are two kinds of objections that a salesman receives on the telephone when requesting an interview:

1. Objection to the telephone call.
2. Objection to the interview.

The salesman might receive many different objections while telephoning for appointments; however, all can be classified as an objection to the call or to the interview. The general technique is used to overcome an objection to either the call or the interview. Your selection of words will vary, as will your vocal delivery, persuasiveness, vitality, energy, inflection, emotional color, pacing, and timing.

For example, "Not in the market" might be answered with a question technique to smoke out the real resistance back of that statement. "Can't you tell me over the phone" might be answered with a disarming, persuasive statement, followed by a request for an agreement on a minor point, rather than on an appointment.

TECHNIQUE IN OVERCOMING OBJECTIONS

The technique of overcoming objections for life underwriters is similar to the technique of any other salesman. Listen to the prospect without any preconceived notions, if possible. What is he saying? Think of the statement or question in terms of the prospect, his needs, desires, goals, and objectives. Answer his statement or objection in this way:

A. Agree sincerely with the prospect. If you cannot agree with his statement, you can agree with his right to make that statement. This builds ego immediately and gives the prospect a feeling of security.

B. Gently switch from the prospect's objection to an interesting benefit or advantage of your plan, or idea, or service. Or you might, depending on his previous statement, give an interesting benefit to be derived by granting an interview.

C. Make time attractive to the prospect. Minimize time, especially if you ask for a "fact-finding" interview.

D. Ask for the appointment immediately after the first three steps have been put into action. Your request for an appointment is a direct suggestion for the prospect to act.

INSURANCE OBJECTIONS

Here are a few of the standard everyday objections that life underwriters receive in telephoning for appointments:

I'm too busy.
Not interested.
I've already got it.
Don't need any.
Not in the market.
No money now.
Have to pay debts first.

Got a friend in the business.
Send it to me in the mail.
You'd be wasting your time.
Have to talk to my partner.
Have to talk to my wife.
I've got a broker.
Tell me over the phone.

ANSWERS TO OBJECTIONS

Here are some answers to objections. Most of these answers will serve as a guide to readers who wish to perfect their technique in overcoming objections.

"Can't you tell me over the phone?"

Phillip D. Swanz, of Midwestern United Life of Fort Wayne, Indiana, says: "I'm sorry, Mr. Brown, but your business is too important for me to attempt to discuss it over the phone. It will take twenty-two minutes for me to show this idea to you and how it can save money for you. Would the morning or the afternoon be more convenient for you?"

"Is this insurance?"

Alfred Aiton, manager of Acacia Mutual Life, Oakland, California, says: "That's an interesting question, Mr. Johnson. It is insurance, but I don't know of any other way to make a favorable tax treatment work to the advantage of your company and its key executives. Do you know of any other way?"

"Can't you send it to me in the mail?"

Mrs. Verda Hoffman, of General American Life, St. Louis, Missouri, answers in this way: "I'll be glad to, Mr. Jones; however, it will be necessary for me to get some information from you first. It will take seven minutes for me to get this information. Which would be better for you, the morning or the afternoon?"

"It sounds like a good idea but I can't do anything now."

Lou Schrepel, of American National Insurance Company, Oakland, California, says: "That decision is entirely up to you, Mr. Winters. My purpose in calling is to request the courtesy of twenty-two minutes to show you the highlights of this plan. Then you can determine whether or not it might be of value to you. Which is better for you, the first of the week or the latter part?"

QUESTION TECHNIQUE

Howard J. Richard, C.L.U., of New York Life in Boston, Massachusetts, believes that questions are the only way you can determine whether the objection is real or fancied. If the objection is real, then Howard complies with the wishes of the prospect. If the prospect does not want to buy any life insurance, Howard would just as soon go on to the next prospect. On the other hand, if the prospect's illusions are purely imaginary, Howard explores them farther with him, until such time as the prospect reasons himself into understanding the illogical background of his thinking.

If the prospect says, "I don't believe in life insurance," Howard replies:

"That's a very interesting point of view. Would you have any objections to telling me why you feel this way?"

Or, if the prospect says, "I can't afford any more life insurance until next fall, "Howard responds in this way:

"May I ask what is going to happen between now and next fall to change your financial picture?"

Clyde E. "Bud" Swift, C.L.U., John Hancock Mutual Life in Knoxville, Tennessee, also answers an objection with a question. If the prospect objects with, "I'm not in the market for insurance right now," Bud replies with:

"In other words, Dr. Moore, you are interested in this plan but feel you are not in the market to buy at this particular time. Is that correct?"

Bud immediately follows the prospect's "yes" with another question that reinforces his first and that motivates the prospect to give an appointment.

Jack Maurer, of First United Life in Indianapolis, Indiana, also answers an objection with a question. Jack has had good results with this one. When the prospect says, "I have a friend in the business," Jack asks:

"How much are you planning to buy from him today?"

Of course, the prospect replies, "None."

There should be a purpose in asking questions other than to get a *yes* response. Recently I worked with an agency that had an approach starting out with three questions. The agents were not getting good responses. As the approach could not be changed, I worked on vocal delivery to soften the bluntness of the questions. Through a change in tempo and tone, with slight pauses before a key word, we made the approach more interesting.

We also worked on imagery, emotional color, pacing, timing, inflection, intonation, emphasis, and contrast until we were able to obtain good results with this approach. A flexible voice is essential in telephoning to communicate nuances of emotion and thought to the prospect and to provide the agent with the means to reveal effectively his own personality in speaking.

PROSPECTS SELDOM SAY "NO"

Last year I gave a Sales Workshop on Telephone Technique at the London Life Insurance Conference in Niagara Falls, Canada. During the program I made the statement that very few prospects actually say "no" to an underwriter on the telephone. After the program, an underwriter told me about his interesting experience with the word "no" in telephoning. This agent had left his city where he was well-known and moved to a city in northern Canada where he was not known. He kept a record of his "cold" calls and objections for one year. During that year, he asked eight hundred persons for an appointment. There were many objections, of course, but only two persons out of eight hundred said "no."

PROSPECT EFFECTIVELY

The best way to reduce objections or circumvent them is to prospect effectively. Jack Wardlaw, regional manager of Philadelphia Life in Raleigh, North Carolina, doesn't receive any objections to his calls. Jack sends out 30,000 birthday cards each year, advertises in good taste, gives excellent service, is well-known, and just doesn't get resistance when he asks for an appointment. I told Jack once that it was a good thing he didn't get objections, as he is so busy making speeches at life underwriter programs throughout the country, he doesn't have much time to make calls.

During the first five months of 1962, Jack actually worked hard for about five weeks. In one week, Jack wrote twenty applications. He wrote eight in one day. During the five-week period, he placed over $800,000. Of course, Jack has a wonderful motto that he lives by daily: "Find a need and fill it!"

Karl Bach, of San Francisco, California, seldom receives an objection. There are many reasons, but one is the excellent service that he gives his clients. Karl has an excellent motto that he lives by: "I don't sell insurance, I help you buy it!" This attitude is expressed over the telephone and in the selling interview.

WHY PROSPECT WON'T BUY

Jack Maurer, of Indianapolis, says: "There are two reasons why the prospect won't grant an interview or buy. They are: (1) the reason he gives, and (2) the real reason."

Jack believes if you can learn to find the *real* reason why the prospect objects, you can close the appointment or the sale quickly and effectively.

DEFERENCE TRANSITIONS

Don Stauffer, of Prudential Insurance Company, Oakland, California, says: "There are several ways in which you can dissuade a person from an idea that is to your disadvantage in obtaining an interview or in closing a sale. To perfect a technique you must practice the use of ego-building statements and deference transitions. When the prospect offers resistance, agree sympathetically with him; then disagree, and make your point."

"I can appreciate that a man in your position would be busy; that's why I telephoned."

"I realize that a man in your position would be busy; however, it will take only twelve minutes for you to see this plan and to determine whether or not it might be of value to you."

"That's an interesting question, Mr. Jones; however, it cannot be answered on the telephone. It will take seven minutes to answer that question for you and to show you what this plan is doing for other successful businessmen."

The deference transition, or ego-building statement, gives the prospect a "cushion" while the conversation is switched from a disadvantage to an advantage.

HUMAN NATURE

Whether you memorize your presentation and your answers to objections or read them, they must be delivered with sincerity and honesty. Keep in mind that every human being likes to think that he can make his own decisions and can act independently of others. He will offer less resistance to a well-prepared approach that is based on the study of human nature. The prospect will offer less resistance to answers to objections if he can "save face" and maintain his dignity.

People differ, of course, in the degree to which they accept suggestions or offer resistance to others. However, it is possible to direct the prospect's thoughts and actions through skillful presentations and answers to objections.

The total telephoning process is built upon many skills and abilities—not just one—and no method can be fully effective that fails to take all of them into account. Salesmen can increase their competence by properly directed practice.

Elmer Leterman says, "The sale begins when the customer says 'no'."

BUYERS—
and
HOW
to
HANDLE
THEM

〰〰〰〰〰〰〰〰〰〰〰〰〰〰〰〰〰 PART **II**

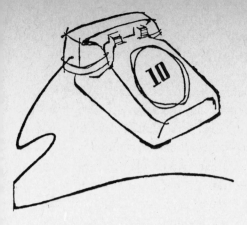

THE MANY KINDS
OF BUYERS

A man convinced against his will is of the same opinion still.
UNKNOWN

SOME TIME AGO I heard Bill Gove speak at a sales rally in Miami that was sponsored by the Sales Executives Club of Miami.

One point that Bill stressed was: "How can I help this other person solve a problem?"

Another point was: "How can I use what I know to help?"

Bill said, "My attitude determines how well I get through to people, how they react to me and my ideas, how long it takes them to accept my ideas and say, 'Yes.' "

If every salesman approached his prospective buyer with these two points in mind, he would be tremendously successful in getting appointments and in closing sales.

THINKING DETERMINES ACTION

Successful telephoning necessitates ability to deal with people. The basic principle of dealing with people is that man has certain wants, needs, and desires that must be satisfied. The successful salesman attempts to influence the behavior of the prospect by appealing to his wants, needs, and desires.

The prospect's thinking is based on his needs, wants, desires,

149

fears, insecurities, and on the picture he has of himself as a person. To a great extent, the thinking of the prospect will determine how he acts or reacts to your conversation. There are many individual differences in the ways your prospects act. Unfortunately, there is no one correct way that you can handle all potential buyers. No two persons are alike, and no two persons are handled in exactly the same way. However, it is possible to develop a technique of handling most people.

TRANSITIONS SOFTEN ANSWERS

Effective deference transitions soften answers to the prospect's objections. There are several ways in which one can turn a disadvantage into an advantage.

1. *The prospect can be exonerated of blame for his idea without reflecting on his judgment.*

    "I must have given you the wrong impression, Mr. Smith, or you would not have made that remark."

2. *You can make a concession to the prospect before you disagree.*

    "You are right, of course, Mr. Smith, but has it occurred to you that this plan could save money for you?"

3. *Get the prospect to deliberate on an idea or to consider the opinion of others.*

    "If I were in your position, Mr. Smith, I would take the opinion of other men in your profession who have used this service for years and who have found it to be satisfactory."

4. *Pay tribute to the prospect before objecting to his viewpoint.*

    "I know you want to do the right thing for your employees, Mr. Smith, or your business associate would not have asked me to get in touch with you about this service."

5. *Restate prospect's idea and get "yes" responses.*

    "In other words, Mrs. Smith, you are interested in having your home painted, but not at this particular time. Is that right?"

    "In other words, Mr. Brown, you are interested in buying a Falcon, but not at this particular time. Is that right?"

    "In other words, Mr. Black, you are interested in saving money but don't feel you could start a savings and investment plan today. Is that correct?"

"In other words, Mr. Brown, you are interested in insurance but not at this particular time. Is that correct?"

6. *Refer to point being objected to as a matter of choice.*

"It is true, Mr. White, that we are an insurance company; however, you may have protection for your family, or retirement for yourself, or both. The choice is yours."

7. *Oppose the prospect's idea with restraint and with courtesy.*

"For some reason, Mr. Jones, your present plan doesn't seem to be the answer to your problem."

Each buyer will respond to you the way his own nervous system works and according to his wants, needs, desires, fears, and insecurities. No two persons will ever respond in exactly the same way. All persons may act differently from others that are in the same category of buyer. If we think maturely about others, realizing that no two persons are alike in all respects, we can develop a "feedback" mechanism of communicating with each person in the way he or she wishes to communicate with others.

The descriptions of the twelve categories of buyers in the following chapters are oversimplified but will help you to identify and classify categories of buyers.

11

THE EXPERT BUYER

THE EXPERT BUYER has a picture of himself as an expert in a buying situation. He will often give the impression that he knows everything about your idea or product. The expert buyer will:

1. Know everything about your idea or product.
2. Bombard you with questions about your idea or product.
3. Dodge your information.
4. Interrupt you frequently.
5. Stop the conversation abruptly.
6. Pay little attention to what you say.

Reassure him that he is an expert:

1. Listen carefully to his comments.
2. Build ego with ego-building statements.
3. Arouse curiosity in the interview.
4. Build suspense for your idea or product.

WHAT TO SAY

Salesman: "Mr. Smith, this is Bill Jones, with Jones' Ford. You and I haven't met; however, we have a mutual friend in Dick Brown, one of your neighbors. Dick recently bought a new Falcon from me and was so pleased with the fine performance and gas economy that he felt you'd be interested in seeing a new Falcon. It will . . . ."

Prospect: (Interrupting) "I want a car with better gas mileage."

Salesman: "I'm glad you brought that up, Mr. Smith, as the Falcon gets up to thirty miles per gallon. Ford proved . . ."

Prospect: "I've been a car owner for a long time and it is my opinion that foreign cars are better."

Salesman: "I can appreciate the fact that you feel that way, Mr. Smith, because other countries have contributed so many worthwhile engineering features. However, you will be amazed at the many unusual features of the Falcon. I can have a new Falcon at your home this evening at 7:00 or 8:00. Which time would be better for you?"

Prospect: "I don't want a scaled-down big car . . . that's what yours is."

Salesman: "I'd feel the same way you do, Mr. Smith, if I had not seen the new Falcons and did not know that every part of this car is entirely new and made just for it. That includes a special economy six-cylinder engine. Would you like to take a demonstration ride in a new Falcon tonight?"

Prospect: "I've been buying cars since I was twenty-one years of age and I know a great deal about them. Your car doesn't have the performance that I want in a car and besides. . . ."

The expert buyer knows everything about your idea or product, and he will tell you that he knows everything about it. Shorten the presentation for the expert buyer and continue to build ego. Answer questions tactfully, diplomatically, with an attempt to close the interview on every objection.

12

THE OPEN-MINDED BUYER

MOST SALESMEN would prefer to sell to the open-minded buyer, encounter few objections, make a quick appointment and later a quick sale. At least, that is the way inexperienced salesmen feel. The master salesman welcomes challenges.

The new salesman looks for an easy sale, while the master salesman looks for the prospect who has a "Do Not Disturb" sign on him.

According to John Dewey, "Open-mindedness may be defined as freedom from prejudice, partisanship, and such other habits as close the mind and make it unwilling to consider new problems and entertain new ideas. But it is something more active and positive than these words suggest. It is very different from empty-mindedness. While it is hospitality to new themes, facts, ideas, questions, it is not the kind of hospitality that would be indicated by hanging out a sign; 'Come right in; there is nobody at home.'"

The open-minded buyer will:

1. Be courteous and friendly.
2. Ask questions pertaining to your idea.
3. Listen attentively to your idea or benefit.

4. Offer sincere objections if he is not interested in your idea, benefit, or product.
5. Be interested in your idea if it appeals to him.
6. Grant interview if it is earned.

Act and talk the way the prospect does.

1. Talk with prospective buyer in a friendly manner.
2. Answer his questions courteously and overcome objections.
3. Don't underestimate open-minded buyer.

WHAT TO SAY

It takes a well-planned approach to handle any type of buyer. The following is an example of the way a realtor at Ebby Halliday Realtors handles an open-minded buyer.

Realtor: "Good morning; Ebby Halliday, Realtors!"

Prospect: "I'd like to have the address of the house you have advertised under Preston Hollow this morning."

Realtor: "Yes! That *is* an interesting property. The wooded grounds must have caught your eye. Are you moving here from the East, where trees are more plentiful?"

Prospect: "No, from Denver, and we have a lot of trees there, too."

Realtor: "Oh, yes, Denver is a beautiful city! We're glad, however, you are moving to Dallas and that our firm will have an opportunity to help you and your family locate. Do you have school-age children?"

Prospect: "Yes, two in elementary, one in college."

Realtor: "Then this house you called about will be right as to the number of bedrooms, and the school situation is excellent. It is quite near the Walnut Hill grade school, also St. Monica. May I ask where you are staying?"

Prospect: "The Ramada Inn."

Realtor: "And your name? Thank you. I'm Jean Shaw. The property is vacant, so it can be shown with no prior appointment. When may I pick you up and show you this colonial and another in the same area?"

Prospect: "Eleven o'clock would be fine with me."

Realtor: "Thank you, Mrs. Smith; I'll see you at 11:00."

In this particular example the realtor withheld her name to see if this was an inquiry call on an ad or a sign. She gave the prospect information before requesting information in return.

13

THE INDIVIDUALISTIC BUYER

THE AMERICAN COLLEGE DICTIONARY gives one definition of an individual as: "Distinguished by peculiar and marked characteristics; exhibiting individuality: a highly individual style."

The American College Dictionary gives one definition of individualism as: "The pursuit of individual rather than common or collective interests; egoism."

These definitions seem to express some of the characteristics and traits of an individualistic buyer.

Many salesmen feel that an individualistic buyer must sell himself or have the illusion that he is selling himself.

The individualistic buyer will:

1. Refuse the appointment quickly.
2. Give reason sometimes for his action in an abrupt manner.
3. Talk about himself or think about himself.
4. Talk about his business or his interests.
5. Not listen to you attentively.
6. Not promise to buy but will often say that he will look at your plan, product, etc., but that he won't promise to buy.

Let him sell himself:

1. Build ego with deference transitions or ego-building statements.
2. Ask questions that will stimulate his thinking.
3. Listen attentively but don't interrupt.
4. Appeal to his individuality.

In Sales Workshops for salesmen and for management, we frequently take a buyer category as a workshop problem to learn how to communicate more effectively with that buyer category. I recently worked with the Michigan management of Midwestern United Life Insurance Company on the individualistic buyer as a workshop problem. Here are some of the questions, objections, and answers that were given during this work-out.

Charles T. Davis, one of the regional sales managers, started the discussion by giving a telephone approach that gave us a pattern to follow.

"Mr. Brown, this is 'Chuck' Davis, of Midwestern United Life. My company has designed an unusual plan for saving money. Are you interested in saving money?"

The supervisors and managers teamed up for role-playing, with one man assuming the role of an individualistic buyer and the other man assuming the role of the salesman.

Dan Wagner, Kalamazoo, asked: "Is this life insurance?"

His partner, Don Sanderson, Kalamazoo, answered: "Only if you die; then you'd need it, wouldn't you?"

Glen Churchill, Detroit, asked: "Can't you tell me what this is over the phone?"

His partner, Bill Oliver, Detroit, answered: "I'll be glad to, Mr. Churchill; however, it will save your valuable time if I show this plan to you. It will take only twelve minutes."

George Knight, of Holt, said: "I don't believe in life insurance."

His partner, Fred Baker, Lansing, replied: "You do believe in saving money, don't you?"

Gerald Brown, of Ada, said: "I'm already saving money."

His partner, Harold Eller, Grand Rapids, answered: "Have you saved all of the money you intend to spend someday?"

Charles Gross, Detroit, said: "I can't save any money."

His partner, Fred Failla, regional manager, said: "If I can show you how to save some money, would you be interested?"

Ross Emrick, Bay City, said: "I can't save any money out of my paycheck."

His partner, Steve Sadlak, Saginaw, asked: "Do you believe there will come a day when your paycheck will stop?"

A few suggestions on asking questions are:

1. Do not ask questions that serve no purpose. When you ask a question make certain that you can ask another related question that will reinforce your previous question.
2. Do not ask questions that will have a tendency to irritate the prospect.
3. Do not ask questions unless you have a feeling that you can control the answers.
4. Ask questions that will give the prospective buyer an opportunity to talk about himself, or his business, or both.
5. Ask questions that will give you the opportunity of going in one direction—on one track—to the close.

14

THE INDECISIVE BUYER

THE INDECISIVE BUYER has been described by many salesmen as a "fence sitter." In other words, he might be described as a person sitting on a fence, not knowing which way to jump.

It is extremely painful in most cases for an indecisive buyer to make a decision. Many salesmen tell me they simply have to make the decision for this type of buyer.

REQUEST FOR RENTAL

Here is a call that every office gets with a fair degree of regularity in the real estate business. A suggestion is made by Fred Jenkins as to one way of turning this rental into a buyer.

It is difficult to detect an indecisive buyer from the printed page, as much of their personality is detected by their hesitancy of speech and by their tone of voice.

Fred: "Good morning! Fred W. Jenkins; this is Fred Jenkins."

Mrs. Brown: "This is Mrs. Harry Brown. Do you have any five-room houses for rent . . . or any six-room houses?"

Fred: "I wish we did, Mrs. Brown, but perhaps I can help you anyway. How much rent do you feel you can pay?"

Mrs. Brown: "I really don't know exactly. I don't think we could pay over $125 or $150 for a house."

Fred: "Would you mind telling me about the size of your family, Mrs. Brown?"

Mrs. Brown: "Well, we have two children, Dick and Patricia. Patricia is the older and will start to school this year."

Fred: "Mrs. Brown, here is an idea that might be of interest to you. We have a three-bedroom colonial, not too far from the Westwood Grade School. That would be an excellent school for Patricia. After a down payment, you can carry it for about $110 a month, which is $40 to $50 a month less than it would be if it were rented."

Mrs. Brown: "That sounds wonderful, but you see my husband doesn't earn enough money to buy a house. We only have about $3,000 in the bank, and that isn't enough for a down payment, is it?"

Fred: "Don't worry, Mrs. Brown, about the down payment. I'll take care of all the details for you and your husband. I suggest that we arrange an appointment this evening so we can discuss this colonial. Would 7:00 or 8:00 be better for you and your husband?"

Mrs. Brown: "I'll have to ask my husband. I know that he wants a house, and it would be good for the children, but I'll have to ask him and call you back."

Fred: "That's perfectly all right, Mrs. Brown. May I ask what time your husband gets home from work?"

Mrs. Brown: "Around 6:00 o'clock."

Fred: "That's fine, I can be at your apartment at 7:00 this evening and we can ask him together. May I please have your address?"

The indecisive buyer will:

1. Hedge and stall without any good reason to do so.
2. Be evasive, unable to make a decision.
3. Will want to talk to someone else.

You will be able to make an appointment quickly if you will:

1. Agree with the prospective buyer but make a definite switch to an advantage of your plan or idea.
2. Offer concrete suggestions to solve the problems.
3. Don't give too many "choices" of ideas.
4. Don't give too many "choices" of time.
5. Agree that the person should talk to someone else. Switch and give this person the opportunity of having you present to take care of the details and to be of assistance to them.
6. Control the interview by definiteness in your tone of voice and in your manner.

The indecisive buyer will respond to firmness and to decisive action, because it is difficult for this type of buyer to be firm and to be decisive.

15

THE TIMID BUYER

THE DICTIONARY defines the word *timid* as: "Subject to fear; easily alarmed; timorous; shy."

In discussing this type of buyer with a psychologist, we learn that this type of buyer will waver back and forth in an effort to make a decision, either to grant the appointment or not to grant the appointment. We also learn that in many cases, this type of buyer has a great hostility toward a salesman or another person and will get revenge by changing his or her mind after the appointment has been granted or after the sale has been consummated.

The timid buyer will:

1. Voice a mild objection.
2. Agree with you easily.
3. Switch back to his first decision or to another decision.
4. Waver back and forth; then grant the appointment.
5. Forget the appointment.
6. Show fear and hostility toward salesman.

In some cases the buyer will not show hostility, but his attitude will affect the sale of a product or plan.

Many salesmen tell me they become friends with this type of buyer immediately. They feel that, when this type of buyer likes them, they can do a better job in making a sale, and that the timid buyer will not change his mind after the sale has been made.

Salesman: "Mrs. Johnson, this is Tom Brown, with the Ajax Air Conditioning Company. Have you a moment to speak on the phone?"

Mrs. Johnson: "Well, I suppose so."

Salesman: "Mrs. Johnson, the purpose of my call is to inquire if you folks have air conditioning in your home?"

Mrs. Johnson: "No, we don't have it. We've been thinking about getting it but just haven't gotten around to it."

Salesman: "I'm glad that you haven't gotten around to it, Mrs. Johnson, because my company has just designed a new air conditioner which fits right into the window of any room in your home and doesn't require any installation. It can be moved from room to room very easily, which increases the comfort of the entire family. It will take thirty minutes to show this air conditioner to you and your family and to show how you can have a cool, comfortable home during the summer when the temperature soars. Which would be the better time for you to see this air conditioner, the day or the evening?"

Mrs. Johnson: "Well, I'd have to ask my husband about it. Besides, we might not be able to take it, and I wouldn't want you to make a trip unless we could take it."

Salesman: "That's perfectly all right, Mrs. Johnson. I'd like to have you and your husband see it and decide for yourselves whether it would be of value to you. It is economical to own and homeowners tell us there is a considerable saving in money, plus the convenience of being able to use it in the room where it is needed most. What time does your husband get home from work?"

Mrs. Johnson: "My husband gets home around 5:00, but I'm not sure he will be able to take it. He has mentioned that he wants one though. . . ."

Salesman: "The decision to take this air conditioner is entirely up up to you and your husband, Mrs. Johnson. I'll show it to you this afternoon at 5:00; if you folks are interested, fine; if not, that's part of my job. I'd like to double-check your address, if I may. Is it 502 South Maple Drive?"

This particular salesman obtained the interview by being interested in the prospective buyer and her family and their comfort. He let her know that her decision would be final. He gave her a no-strings-attached offer.

You can make appointments with the timid buyer if you will:

1. Listen sympathetically to his or her objections.
2. Keep on one track, by continuing to ask for the appointment.
3. Show advantage of your product, or show the benefit of your product.
4. Be friends with your prospective buyer. Express warmth and friendliness in your voice and manner.
5. Keep the prospective buyer feeling as comfortable as possible.
6. Speak in a decisive tone of voice. You will evoke a better response in your prospect.

If you speak in a timid, indecisive, fearful tone of voice, your prospect will be affected by your voice and will not respond in an affirmative way.

16

THE LOGICAL BUYER

THE LOGICAL BUYER will usually seek additional information about you, your firm, your idea, your product, the benefit to him. He will usually have an alert, inquiring mind and will ask more questions than most other types of buyers.

The logical buyer will ask:

1. For more information about you, your firm, your plan.
2. How the plan works? How the idea works?
3. For more information over the phone.
4. That information be sent to him in the mail.
5. Who had used your services, product, etc.
6. What were the results from using your services, idea, etc.

The logical buyer will listen to sound reasoning and has an open mind for a good idea or plan that will benefit him or his family or his employees or his firm.

Listen attentively to his remarks and to his questions.

1. Create interest for your plan or idea. Give him some idea as to how your plan or idea might benefit him.
2. Build some suspense for the interview. Do not divulge your entire plan or idea or details over the phone.
3. If possible, do not send a detailed outline of your plan or idea before your sales interview.
4. Appeal to his sound reasoning.

DIRECT MAIL

C. Armel Nutter, Jr., manager of the Nutter Mortgage Service in Philadelphia, sends several types of letters to potential customers. Here is one sample letter and an example of a telephone call that was made to a logical buyer.

Mr. John Doe
129 King Street
Suburbs, Pennsylvania

Dear Mr. Doe:
We observe from recent Dodge Reports that you are planning construction of a shopping center in your town.

For many years we have arranged mortgage financing for this type of construction and believe we can be of assistance to you.

We would appreciate your noting on the copy of this letter, which can be returned in the enclosed prepaid envelope, when it will be convenient for us to discuss this with you personally; or if you would prefer to telephone for an appointment, we shall be glad to arrange it.

We await your pleasure and the opportunity of serving you.

Very sincerely yours,
C. Armel Nutter, Jr., *Manager*
NUTTER MORTGAGE SERVICE

CAN.JR:laf
Enclosure

Armel follows the letter with a telephone call that goes something like this:

"Mr. Doe, this is Armel Nutter, of Nutter Mortgage Service. Have you a moment to speak on the phone?" (Waits for reply.)

"Mr. Doe, recently I mailed a letter to you regarding our mortgage financing. Did you receive it?" (Waits for reply.)

If Mr. Doe did not receive the letter or does not remember receiving it, the conversation will go like this:

Mr. Doe: "No, I didn't receive it. What's it all about?"

Armel: "That's why I telephoned, Mr. Doe; the letter was important. It briefly stated that we have arranged mortgage financing for the type of construction you are planning for a shopping center in your town. It will take thirty minutes for me to give you the highlights of our service and for you to determine its value to you. Which would be better for you, the morning or the afternoon?"

Mr. Doe: "Have you done business with someone in my town whom I might know?"

Armel: "Yes, Mr. Doe. I believe you would know Mr. Stanley Powers, of the ABC Company. His address is 502 National Bank Building. Would you like to have his telephone number also?"

Mr. Doe: "No, thanks, I'll get it here. Could you tell me some of the details of your services over the phone?"

Armel: "I'd be glad to, Mr. Doe; however, it will save your valuable time if we arrange an interview with you and your associates. In this way we can make a formal presentation of our services and give each of you gentlemen the opportunity of asking questions about our services. Which would be the better time for you, the morning or the afternoon?"

Mr. Doe: "The morning is the best time for us. Could you be in my office tomorrow morning at 9:30?"

Armel: "Yes, Mr. Doe. I can be there at 9:30. Thank you."

17

THE COMPLAINER BUYER

THE COMPLAINER BUYER can be handled expertly by the person who realizes that the complaints are being given without any thought as to the person, situation, or the firm. The person who answers the telephone is in many cases the target for the buyer's complaints.

The complainer will:

1. Complain immediately and seek your sympathy.
2. Be inattentive to what you say.
3. Be frustrated and blame you or the firm.
4. Project frustration, problems, troubles upon you.

Here are some suggestions for handling the complainer buyer:

1. Be sympathetic and agree with the buyer.
2. Establish understanding with him or her.
3. Agree that the complaint is probably justified.
4. Assume blame immediately.
5. Take action quickly to handle the matter.
6. Do not become emotionally involved in the complaints.

THE COMPLAINER COMPLAINS

Mrs. Home Executive ordered some towels that were advertised in the daily newspaper from the Telephone Selling Department of the local department store. Towels of the wrong color were delivered to her by mistake. Seeing the wrong color, Mrs. Home Executive makes a quick telephone call to the store.

Mrs. Jones: "I ordered some towels from your store and received them today but they are the wrong color. I tried to catch your driver, but he hurried off before I could tell him my towels were the wrong color. I want you to send him back to get these towels. *I don't want them.*"

Saleswoman: "I'm very sorry you received the wrong color. May I ask who is calling, please?"

Mrs. Jones: "My name is Mrs. Robert Jones. I wanted those towels for some special guests we are having this week end, but the color is wrong and I don't want them."

Saleswoman: "I don't blame you at all, Mrs. Jones. If they are the wrong color you would not have any use for them. May I ask your address?"

Mrs. Jones: "I've been trading at your store for ten years. Surely you would know my address by this time. Every time I place an order and it arrives, there is something wrong with it."

Saleswoman: "I'm sorry to hear that, Mrs. Jones. The purpose of asking your address was to try to get your towels to you as soon as possible. Is your address 610 Corona Drive?"

Mrs. Jones: "Yes, that's right. I'm glad you got something straight. I can't imagine sending the wrong color, unless your clerk is color-blind."

Saleswoman: "May I ask what kind of towels you ordered, and the color, Mrs. Jones?"

Mrs. Jones: "I ordered Brand X with three brown towels and three beige, with washcloths to match. You sent some blue towels to me, and there isn't a blue bedroom in my house."

Saleswoman: "Naturally, you would have no use for blue towels then, Mrs. Jones. We can have your towels to you by noon tomorrow; that's Thursday. Would that be soon enough?"

Mrs. Jones: "Yes, my guests don't arrive until Saturday. I'll send the other towels back by your driver."

Saleswoman: "Thank you, Mrs. Jones. We will appreciate your courtesy in doing that. You mentioned that other items had not been satisfactory. May I ask what they were, so I can take care of them for you at this time?"

Mrs. Jones: "Oh, that was five years ago. Your store sent the wrong kind of kitchen curtains to me, but they changed them for me. Everything has been taken care of."

Saleswoman: "I'm glad to hear that everything has been taken care of satisfactorily, Mrs. Jones. Is there any way that I may be of service to you at this time?"

Mrs. Jones: "No, thank you for sending the towels. Good-by."

Saleswoman: "Good-by, Mrs. Jones."

18

THE PRICE BUYER

ARTHUR HOLTZMAN, Jr. and Sr., invited me to give a Sales Workshop on Telephone Technique for their Mutual of Omaha Agency in Rochester, New York, some time ago. We had a stimulating session of work-outs on the twelve buyer categories.

Harold Redmond gave an excellent performance in handling the price buyer. Incidentally, the price buyer bothers more salesmen than probably any other type of buyer.

Many salesman feel that the price buyer does not have the ability to pay, and they leave him alone when they detect their prospect is a price buyer. Nothing could be farther from the truth.

In many cases the price buyer has money to pay. Psychologists have said that many persons who have been deprived of love and affection in their early years in life often pay more attention to money than other types of buyers. Many price buyers have the ability to pay.

The price buyer will:

1. Ask about cost.
2. Ask how much he can save with your product or plan.
3. Say that he can't afford it.
4. Talk about hard times.
5. Seldom ask about quality.
6. Seldom ask about service.

Here are some suggestions that Harold Redmond followed in handling the price buyer:

1. Reassure buyer about price.
2. Change price to "saving."
3. Don't give price over the telephone.
4. Be warm and friendly.
5. Be sympathetic about buyer's concern over rising costs, inflation, etc.

BUYER'S REACTION

Harold: "Hello, Mr. Jones. This is Harold Redmond, with Mutual of Omaha. Do you have a moment to speak on the phone?"

Mr. Jones: "Just a moment. What is it?"

Harold: "Mr. Jones, I was over talking to Bill Brown the other day. During the course of the conversation your name was mentioned, and I asked if I could stop to make your acquaintance. I'm planning to stop by your house this week, but thought I'd call you first to see if Monday at 6:00 or Tuesday at 8:00 would be more convenient for you. Which would be better for you, Mr. Jones?"

Mr. Jones: "What is it about, Mr. Redmond?"

Harold: "That is what I want to stop and show you, Mr. Jones. Would Monday be satisfactory, or would Tuesday be better?"

Mr. Jones: "I can't afford to buy anything now."

Harold: "This plan isn't based on the amount of money you have in your pocket, Mr. Jones; besides, the decision to buy is entirely up to you. Is that fair?"

Mr. Jones: "Mr. Redmond, I believe Bill did mention this to me. I am interested in your plan, but before you waste your time in coming over, tell me, how much does it cost?"

Harold: "If I could show you that my plan might save money for you instead of costing anything, would you be interested?"

Mr. Jones: "Yes, if you can show me where there might be a saving, I'm interested."

Harold: "That's fine, Mr. Jones. Which day would be better for you, Monday or Tuesday?"

Mr. Jones: "Tuesday would be all right with me. Around 8:00 o'clock."

Harold: "Thank you, Mr. Jones. I'll see you Tuesday evening at 8:00 o'clock."

Mr. Jones: "Remember this is going to save me money."

Harold: "That's right, Mr. Jones. It will save you money. Thanks very much. Good-by."

19

THE BULLY BUYER

THE BULLY BUYER is frequently disliked by inexperienced salesmen because they do not know how to treat him. The bully is frequently a coward at heart. He will respond to firmness, warmth, strength, and persuasive skills.

The bully buyer might:

1. Be rude or explosive in his remarks.
2. Be abrupt in manner.
3. Try to dominate the conversation.
4. Speak to you in a loud tone of voice.
5. Put you on the defensive.
6. Fight against the appointment.

Here are some of the ways in which salesmen deal with the bully buyer:

1. Be friendly but firm in manner and tone.
2. Give praise to the bully through deference transitions.
3. Build ego and agree with him.
4. Demonstrate strength against his loud voice and abrupt manner.
5. Do not be apologetic to him.
6. Use reasoning, and appeal to needs, wants, desires.

WHAT TO SAY

Jack: "Mr. Green, this is Jack Allen, of Allen's Ford. Do you have a moment to speak on the phone?"

Green: (abrupt manner) "Just a minute. What do you want?"

Jack: "Dick Evans recently bought a new Falcon from me and was so pleased with the fine performance and gas economy that he felt you'd be interested in seeing one, too. Would you be interested in a car that gives you up to thirty miles per gallon?"

Green: (abrupt voice) "I'm not in the market for a car."

Jack: "In other words, Mr. Green, you are interested in a car that gives you up to thirty miles per gallon, but feel you are not in the market at this time. Is that correct?"

Green: "That's correct."

Jack: "When do you feel you will be in the market for a new car, Mr. Green?"

Green: "Probably after the first of the year."

Jack: "May I ask what kind of car you are driving at this time?"

Green: "This wouldn't be for me but for my wife."

Jack: "If this is a second car, you would probably be interested in economy. Is that right?"

Green: "Yes, but my wife would want good performance, too."

Jack: "This is where the Falcon is ahead, Mr. Green; but you'll have to drive the new Falcon to see that it is ahead in performance as well as economical in gas mileage. I can have a new Falcon at your home at 6:00 o'clock this evening, if you and Mrs. Green would like to take a ride in it. Would 6:00 o'clock be all right, or would 7:00 be better for you?"

Green: "Well, it won't hurt to take a ride in it to see if that is the car Mrs. Green would want. Have a car at my home at 7:00 o'clock sharp."

Jack: "Thank you, Mr. Green. May I have your address?"

20

THE EMOTIONAL BUYER

WHILE INTERVIEWING Bob Saatz, top salesman at General Development Corporation in Miami, I asked if he qualified the prospective buyer during the telephone conversation.

Bob's answer was a definite, "Yes." Bob added, "A good salesman will recognize a suspect or a prospect quickly during the telephone conversation."

My next question was: "Which of the twelve categories of buyers would you prefer to sell."

"The emotional buyer," Bob replied. He added quickly, "I like to sell the prospect through an emotional appeal. Perhaps that is because I am emotional about the benefits and about selling."

The emotional buyer will:

1. Be annoyed at your telephone call for a moment.
2. Give a quick objection to your telephone call.
3. Be inattentive when you mention some of your sales points.
4. Talk about himself or herself.
5. Ask about his or her benefits, gain, etc.
6. Be motivated through emotional appeals.

To obtain an appointment, you may:

1. Appeal to the prospective buyer's ego, or vanity, or both.
2. Appeal to pride and imitation.
3. Arouse curiosity for the interview.
4. Use third party influence.

WHAT TO SAY

Miss Hall: "Hello."

Bob: "Miss Hall, this is Bob Saatz, of General Development. I had the pleasure of selling Juanita Smith some property recently, and she suggested that I get in touch with you. Miss Smith felt that you might like to have the same opportunity of making an investment in Port Malabar that she had. The purpose of my call is to request the courtesy of an appointment to show you what is going on at Port Malabar, the fastest growing city in Florida. Which would be better for you, the day or the evening?"

Miss Hall: "I don't know whether I'd be interested or not."

Bob: "May I ask if you have ever considered an investment of this type?"

Miss Hall: "No, I haven't considered this particular type of investment; however, I am looking for some kind of investment."

Bob: "May I ask the type of investment you had in mind, Miss Hall?"

Miss Hall: "Well, I wanted something for retirement. I will retire in five years, maybe sooner: I'd like to get started on some type of investment for retirement. I know one thing—I want to live in Florida when I retire."

Bob: "Then you would be very much interested in Port Malabar, our fastest growing city in Florida. I'd like to show you Port Malabar, so you can see what is going on there."

Miss Hall: "I want a good investment for my money, and I might add that I don't have very much capital at this time. I will have money available soon for an investment."

Bob: "That's perfectly all right, Miss Hall. You can make an investment of this type without tying up any of your capital. I'll take care of all of the details for you. Which day would be the most convenient for you, a day through the week or Saturday?"

Miss Hall: "Saturday would be the best time for me."

Bob: "I will be leaving for Port Malabar at 8:30 on Saturday, Miss Hall. Is that a convenient time for you?"

Miss Hall: "Well, that is early, but I can make it."

Bob: "That will be fine, Miss Hall. Would you please give me your address?"

Miss Hall: "Certainly. It is 342 Main Street."

Bob: "Thank you. I'll see you Saturday then at 8:30, Miss Hall. Good-by."

Miss Hall: "Good-by."

21

THE STUBBORN BUYER

THE STUBBORN BUYER is a good client, after you obtain the appointment and make the sale.

The stubborn buyer will:

1. Give abrupt objections.
2. Be emphatic about his objection, will stall, or make excuses.
3. Fight against the appointment.
4. Ask dominating questions or make dominating statements.

The master salesman will show the stubborn buyer advantages of arranging an appointment. He will:

1. Agree with the prospective buyer.
2. Build ego.
3. Adopt a customer-you attitude.
4. Arouse curiosity.
5. Build suspense for the interview.

HOW TO DO IT

Charlie Gibbs, of Mutual Benefit Life of New Jersey in Los Angeles, uses nineteen tax-saving ideas. Charlie's approach is:[1] "I would like to bring to your attention, Mr. Jackson, nineteen tax-saving ideas that I have found for businesses. For example, you can get dollars out of the corporation without income tax (pause) legally. You can let your business carry your personal life insurance for you. You can let your business pay all of your family's medical expenses. It will take a few minutes for me to show these nineteen tax-saving ideas to you. Then I can determine which will be of value to you. Would the morning or the afternoon be more convenient for you?"

Mr. Jackson: "How can your tax-saving ideas help me?"

Charlie: "Mr. Jackson, I can show you how to put your money into your pocket instead of Uncle Sam's. This can be done after talking to you. All I ask is three minutes of your time and I'll come in with my watch in my hand. I promise to leave at the end of that time unless you ask me to stay. Is that fair?"

Mr. Jackson: "That's fair, but how long will it take for you to determine which of these ideas will be of value to me? I want to know before I give an appointment."

Charlie. "It would take one hour for me to get the information that I would need; however, it would take only three minutes to show these ideas to you. Would you prefer to make this an hour interview, so I can get the facts at that time?"

Mr. Jackson: "Can you give them to me over the phone?"

Charlie: "I'm sorry, Mr. Jackson, but all of these don't apply to you; some of them do. It would be a waste of your valuable time for us to discuss all nineteen of these because there are a lot that wouldn't fit you. So I suggest that we arrange an interview so I can obtain from you the information that I would need, which I can do in the maximum of one hour."

Mr. Jackson: "Then where do we go from there?"

---

[1] Reprinted through the courtesy of *Insurance Field,* January 20, 1961.

Charlie: "That's a good question, Mr. Jackson. Then I'll go back to my office and study that information and check it with these ideas. Then I'll come back, and in one hour I can give you all of my recommendations. If we find that nothing need be changed, you will have a lot of peace of mind in knowing that everything is up-to-date. But if we find something wrong, you will want to correct it immediately. Now you are gambling two hours of your time, and if you feel, at the end of those two hours, that my ideas are not worth the time, I'll pay you double what you earn in two hours."

Mr. Jackson: "That's a good deal."

Charlie: "I say this, Mr. Jackson, because I have never yet come to that man who could not be helped by some of these ideas. Which time would be more convenient for you, the morning or the afternoon?"

Mr. Jackson: "The morning is better for me. Be here in my office tomorrow morning at nine."

Charlie: "Nine o'clock is fine with me, Mr. Jackson. Thank you for your courtesy. Good-by."

Mr. Jackson: "Good-by."

22

THE FLIRT BUYER

IT IS DIFFICULT in some cases to distinguish the flirt buyer from the open-minded buyer. The difference between these two buyers is that the open-minded buyer will listen to a good idea, will grant an interview, and will make a purchase, if the idea or product appeals to him or to her.

The flirt buyer, in most cases, does not have any intention of buying the product, of using the service, or of responding to the idea. The flirt buyer may not be in the market for the product, service, or benefits of the plan, but will grant an interview to the salesman.

Some salesmen call this type of prospect the "lonely" buyer. He likes to talk but seldom makes an investment in your product.

The flirt buyer will listen to your story about your product on the telephone, or at the door, or in the interview. Some of these people actually enjoy meeting the salesman, hearing about new products or plans on the market, and are curious about your product. They are flattering to talk to and are probably good conversationalists, but they waste the salesman's time. The flirt buyer will:

182

1. *Be courteous and friendly.*
   "I'm glad you called. My husband and I have been talking about getting a new vacuum cleaner."
2. *Be receptive to your call and to your suggestions.*
   "Yes, I would like to see a demonstration of the new vacuum cleaner."
3. *Listen attentively to your story on the telephone.*
   "Your vacuum cleaner sounds like it is what I have been looking for and need."
4. *Will discuss your product enthusiastically.*
   "Yes, I've heard that Brand X does clean more thoroughly than other cleaners."
5. *Will give you an opportunity to convince her of the features of your product.*
   "You're probably right. It will save wear and tear on my rugs and will save money."
6. *Will leave time open and will seldom make a definite appointment.*
   "I'm at home all day. Any time you come over would be all right."

WHAT TO DO

Pin the flirt buyer to specific time for the interview, and ask questions to determine her interest and need.

"May I ask how many rooms you have carpeted?"
"May I ask if you rent your home or own it?"

1. Arrange a definite time for the demonstration or interview.
2. Ask questions to determine whether the prospect is interested, and to what extent.
3. Ask qualifying questions, if possible, to determine whether you have a prospect or a suspect.
4. Prolong the telephone conversation until you have an opportunity to listen to the person's words, phrases, and voice. Perhaps you can determine that the person is a flirt buyer instead of an open-minded buyer.

The purpose of the telephone is to make appointments, but you can also qualify your prospective buyer and save unnecessary time and expense by eliminating suspects on the telephone.

MODERN
USE
of
the
TELEPHONE

ꙮꙮꙮꙮꙮꙮꙮꙮꙮꙮꙮꙮꙮꙮꙮꙮꙮꙮꙮꙮ **PART III**

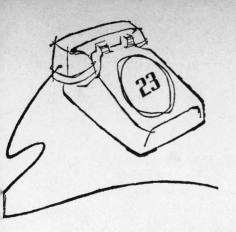

MODERN

TELEPHONE SHOPPING

Progress is the activity of today and the assurance of to-morrow.

RALPH WALDO EMERSON

ALL RETAILERS are continuously looking for answers to two vital questions:

1. How to increase sales?
2. How to control expenses?

The Telephone Selling Department (TSD) is a new concept for increased sales at no increase in inventory and little capital investment. If properly planned, engineered, conducted, and promoted, a modern Telephone Selling Department can increase sales and control expenses.

J. C. Porter, vice-president, Sales, The Robert Simpson Company, Ltd. in Toronto, says: "We have actively promoted telephone shopping for many years. We have found that the convenience of a good telephone shopping service has made many new friends and customers for Simpson's. It is definitely 'plus' business here."

CHANGES IN RETAILING

Retailing has changed within the past several years. A broader merchandising approach is needed to expose the consumer oftener

187

to department store merchandise. Aggressive telephone shopping programs are needed to make buying easier for the customer.

The population is shifting to the suburbs; however, branch stores are only a partial solution. Downtown stores are too far away but your Telephone Selling Department is only five to ten *seconds* away by telephone. Downtown driving, traffic, parking, and other transportation problems are cutting into store profits, but the telephone can bring the downtown store to the customers.

Today the consumer is buying more department store items elsewhere. The telephone can expose the customer oftener to department store merchandise. It can speed up the frequency of sales contacts by making buying easier. If you give your potential customers sufficient product information and the right telephone number to call, they will be your regular customers.

Your Telephone Selling Department can help to solve the problem of having too many clerks when they are not needed and too few when they are needed. Your telephone can help spread business activity more evenly and stimulate off-hour buying. Through carefully timed promotions and newspaper specials, you can offer bargains for telephone orders at certain times during the day and after closing hours. All of these problems point to two basic related needs—more volume and profits.

SURVEY OF A STORE

National Analysts, Inc., of Philadelphia, was asked to conduct a survey. Using a comprehensive questionnaire, over two thousand Baltimore housewives were interviewed. The C & P Telephone Company of Maryland also made a thorough study of Stewart's in Baltimore. Here are the conclusions indicated by the survey and study of its telephone shopping operation:

1. There are over 200,000 women in Baltimore who either work, have pre-school children, or are chronically too ill to shop in person. This is one in three.
2. For every eight automobiles in the downtown area, there is only *one* parking space.

3. Forty-four per cent of the women who visited Stewart's and Company during the month before the survey said they did not buy while in the store but many bought by telephone when they got home.
4. Nearly 50 per cent of the customers who preferred Stewart's for in-store shopping preferred another store for telephone shopping.
5. Seventy per cent of the women interviewed disliked store advertising that said, "No phone orders." Another common complaint: "Store number not in ad."

Stewart and Company, with the aid and assistance of the Telephone Company, got under way with a new program.

Telephone "traffic" analyses were made for both the telephone order board and the store's main switchboard. Call volume was plotted by hours, days, weeks, and months.

New methods and practices were introduced—new tally sheets for recording transactions, new results-summary sheets, increased display of the store's telephone number in its advertising, and new procedures regarding referrals, outgoing calls, and suggestive selling.

MODERN TELEPHONE SELLING DEPARTMENT

A modern telephone selling department featuring twenty-four order-taking positions, was set up in a new location that was sound-conditioned and modernized.

New telephone sales personnel were selected and trained under experienced Telephone Company supervision.

Special procedures were instituted to measure the effectiveness of the new telephone selling program. Every telephone sales transaction was recorded. Data from a 20 per cent sample were transferred to punch cards, and summaries, analyses, and validations were run off.

RESULTS OF A PROGRAM

An analysis of the new telephone shopping operation, made over a three-year period, provided some dramatic results:

Telephone shoppers appeared to be the most frequent in-store shoppers as well, and many new telephone customers became new in-store shoppers.

Over-all telephone selling costs (including direct selling costs, delivery, and wrapping) were 50.9 per cent lower than for selling over the counter.

The dollar volume of the average telephone order was 40 per cent higher than that for the average store sale.

Cost of occupancy (including fixtures, utilities, taxes, insurance, and amortization of capital investment) was 28 per cent lower than for the rest of the downtown store.

Returns on telephone sales were only 1.4 per cent higher than those for sales made on the floor of the store.

While Stewart's did promote their telephone shopping service in their advertising, no additional space cost was incurred. Ads were designed so as to accommodate the telephone shopping phone number.

TELEPHONE SALES INCREASED

Other significant results were:

Stewart's order-taking positions were expanded twice to take care of increased telephone sales that year. They increased from sixteen to twenty-four in October and from twenty-four to thirty-six in November.

Specifically, telephone sales volume increased 31.75 per cent over the previous year, and 26.2 per cent the following year.

Total annual sales per telephone sales clerk were 112 per cent higher than for the average store clerk.

Ray Greenhill, Stewart's president said: "Our ratio of telephone sales to gross sales increased from 3.2 per cent to about 10 per cent—well beyond our original objective. Telephone shopping is really paying off for us."

EQUIPMENT AND FACILITIES

Different stores have different needs. These needs depend on the size of the store, volume of business, facilities, store policies, and the aggressiveness of management. Many stores do not require additional equipment but merely a sharpening up of existing facilities; the polishing of communication and sales techniques; the introduction of more efficient methods and procedures; and more effective training of telephone sales people.

But equipment is important and cannot be overlooked. The equipment, privacy panels, conveyor belts, working surfaces, space for reference materials, and other improvements are of great importance to the telephone sales personnel. These improvements will increase telephone sales and profits.

HANDLING TELEPHONE ORDERS

The handling of telephone orders need not be considered a specialized business. Many stores, particularly the smaller ones, do a substantial telephone business without a separate department for this function. However, as the store becomes larger, it is desirable, for many reasons, to centralize its telephone business. This trend has resulted in the modern telephone salesroom with its specialized equipment and highly trained employees, who contribute substantially to the financial welfare of the store. A well-organized Telephone Selling Department program can provide a store with a new department that will outsell any existing department, with no increase in inventory and with very little capital investment.

EQUIPMENT DEPENDS ON STORE NEEDS

The equipment used depends largely on the store's needs and the physical layout of the telephone sales department. Many stores have specially designed positions for taking telephone orders. Some features of order-taking positions considered desirable are:

1. "Privacy" panels that separate clerks and reduce distractions.
2. Adequate working surface for each telephone clerk.
3. Space for each clerk's personal effects.
4. Conveyor belts for forwarding sales checks.
5. Suitable space for reference materials, such as ad tear sheets, catalogs, ad digest, merchandise lists, and other materials.

WORKING TOOLS AND REFERENCE MATERIALS

The telephone shopping clerk must be familiar with all departments and their merchandise. Convenient, accurate reference material must be available to assist her in her work. Her sales performance will be directly proportionate to the completeness of this information and to her ability to translate it into terms the customer will understand.

Some of the working tools and reference materials are:

ad tear sheets
color chart
concession item list
consumption item list
delivery zone guide and schedule
department list—items
desk layout
filing system
item list—departmental
measurement guide

order forms
out-of-stock list
related item list
"returns" practices
sales-tax computation table
sales-tax ruling guide
size chart
special sale item list
store telephone directory
tartan plaid guide

ADVERTISED MERCHANDISE

About 80 per cent of the total orders handled by the telephone sales clerk will be advertised merchandise, so her first point of reference will be tear sheets of current newspaper ads. Tear sheets should go to the telephone shopping supervisor as far in advance of publication as possible. Past experience will enable her to estimate force requirements, based on the type of merchandise advertised and the amount of advertising.

Some larger stores have found it impractical to use tear sheets. These stores use skilled copywriters to digest the ads into printed descriptions. These digests take far less room than tear sheets and are more convenient to handle. Supplementing the tear sheets or ad digests are lists of staples or "never out of stock" items. Many stores print seasonal catalogs, and these, too, should be on hand at each sales position.

The competitive nature of the department store business often causes almost minute-to-minute changes in the reference material. These usually take the form of a "sold out" notice or a change in price. In smaller stores, the telephone shopping supervisor can make appropriate changes on tear sheets or pass the information verbally to her saleswomen. Some large stores have found it practical to project such notices on a screen in front of sales positions.

Adequate reference material costs money and takes time to prepare. But every minute of time and every dollar of expense is usually justified. Lack of material causes too many calls to the selling floors, increased transfer of calls, and more returned merchandise.

TELEPHONE SELLING PERSONNEL

The telephone sales clerk has a highly specialized job to do and should be selected with care. She is the "voice" of your store and represents or misrepresents it every time she takes a call or makes a call.

The six major objectives for a telephone sales clerk are:

Customer service
Sales
Promotion
Accuracy
Courtesy
Tact

The types of customer calls to be handled are:

Sales orders
Merchandise inquiries
Delivery inquiries
Service calls
Returns
Exchanges
Complaints
Adjustments

TRAINING INCREASES PROFITS

Nothing makes telephone shopping "click" so much as well-trained telephone sales people. The telephone clerk has an important sales job to do and a public relations job, too. Training makes all the difference in profits for your store. The Telephone Company will be glad to train your telephone sales personnel to insure bigger profits in your Telephone Selling Department. After the Telephone Company trains your department, your supervisor can maintain the program and increase its effectiveness through close supervision and regular meetings.

THE TELEPHONE SALES CLERK

The telephone sales clerk should be alert to sales opportunities. She should have the ability to listen to the customer with interest, translate her message quickly and accurately, and answer her in such a manner as to evoke a favorable response. She should quickly recognize customer needs and wants. She should be able to establish a rapport quickly with an unseen audience, and to make the customer feel that she is receiving personal attention just as she would if she were making a purchase in the store. The clerk should be able to talk to customers easily, in a cheerful tone of voice, expressing warmth and friendliness, as well as courtesy and tact. She should be able to control her voice while under pressure or stress of business, or during emotional upsets. The customer must never hear the "personal" problems of the telephone clerk in her voice, words, or personality. Emotional and vocal control are requisites of a capable telephone sales clerk.

CLERK MUST KNOW MERCHANDISE

The telephone sales clerk must have the ability to know merchandise, stock conditions, price, and be quick to grasp details and to handle them accurately. She must have an ability to write quickly, accurately, and legibly. She should have a familiarity with the buying needs of the store's customers and an understanding of their needs and problems. She must be aware at all times that she can greatly influence customer attitudes and make sales for the store.

BASIC TOPICS IN TRAINING PROGRAM

No one training program can be presented that would be of maximum value to stores of all sizes and types; however, there are some basic topics that are applicable to every store.

Orientation
Merchandise review
Paper transactions
Telephone practices
Order-board procedures
Learning use of equipment

Learning sales system
Sales techniques
Communication skills
Making outgoing calls
Receiving incoming calls
Public relations practice

C. Virgil Martin, president of Carson Pirie Scott and Company, Chicago, said: "A realistic training program, with specific direction and the best of supervision, is producing excellent sales results in our telephone order department. We at Carson's believe that all employees are members of one team, working for the common goals—prompt, courteous, and reliable service to our customers, good working conditions for employees, and reasonable profit for the company."

DUTIES OF SUPERVISOR

The supervisor is actually a department manager whose sales might be as high, or higher, than those of other large departments in the store. The right person in this job can mean profits for the store. The supervisor can help boost sales among the telephone sales clerks and assure a highly successful telephone shopping department.

Some of the responsibilities of the supervisor are:

1. Conducts personnel interviews.
2. Sets up training programs and requirements.
3. Conducts special training classes.
4. Assigns work schedules.
5. Analyzes force requirements.
6. Reviews advertising activities.
7. Reviews promotion activities.

8. Observes and checks on incoming calls.
9. Maintains information on stock levels.
10. Negotiates changes in policies and procedures.
11. Keeps the department's budgets.
12. Evaluates personnel in view of their performances.

CUSTOMER CONTACT PRACTICE

Practice cases, illustrative of each type of customer call, should be given to telephone sales clerks. After introduction of the subject, principles, methods, and procedures, the clerks should act-out the situations until they become skilled in handling every type of customer contact before they are permitted to handle a call. Encourage each clerk to participate in the role-playing situations, with one clerk assuming the role of a customer and another assuming the role of the clerk. This type of practice will, for the most part, reduce errors with customers and eliminate costly mistakes for the store.

Prepare a series of practice cases for each of the customer calls. New telephone clerks should be trained in small groups. In this way, they are not embarrassed, and the supervisor can pinpoint weaknesses readily and take corrective action. She can evaluate the clerk's performance under simulated working conditions and can help each person to adapt to different customers and to different types of calls.

STEPS TO THE SALE

Introduction—   The telephone sales clerk will practice identifying the store and herself in a natural, conversational, confident tone of voice.
"Good morning; Harris and Harris; Mrs. Lane speaking."

Fact-finding—   She will then obtain information regarding the customer's needs by skillful questioning. "Mrs. Johnson, what is the age of the child you're buying the gift for?"
"Mrs. Wood, what size does your niece wear?"

Recommendations— The clerk should learn at the outset to present an item that will fit the need of the customer, based upon her previous statements or requests for information. Suggestive selling should be stressed to every new clerk, and she should learn how to follow through with tact, diplomacy, accurate judgment, and skill.

"I suggest you also take four of the hand towels that match, Mrs. Sharpe. Would you like two in the brown?"

Answering objections—To answer objections, use a deference transition or an ego-building statement to soften your switch from the customer's objection to your product advantage or to your request for additional information in order to handle a complaint or return.

"I can appreciate that it is more than you planned to spend; however, the hand towels do match the towels you ordered. They add to the attractiveness of your bathroom, and there is a saving, if ordered today. Will four be enough for you, Mrs. Sharpe?"

Closing— Ask for the order. Get agreement from the customer on minor points.

"Will four be enough?"

"Would you like all in one color, or would you like to have one of each color?"

"Would you like to have the fan picked up and replaced with the larger model?"

"Which would you prefer, the large or the medium size?"

"Which would you prefer, the brown or the black?"

"Which would you prefer, the $3.98 or the $4.98 price?"

The Telephone Company has a film and associated film clips *Four Steps to Sales* that will be of assistance to telephone sales clerks. The film can be obtained from the local Telephone Company representative.

PRACTICE SALE

Employee: "Good morning; Winslow Department Store; Mrs. Moore speaking."

Customer: "I'd like to order some towels that you had advertised in the paper last night."

Employee: "I'll be glad to send them to you. Do you wish them charged?"

Customer: "Yes, charge it, please. My name is Mrs. Thomas Babcock, 138 S. Central Street, Zone 23."

Employee: "Mrs. Babcock, what color towels do you wish?"

Customer: "Is the brown a dark shade or a light shade?"

Employee: "We have the towels in a rich dark brown or in a light brown. Both are very attractive."

Customer: "Send me three of each, the dark brown and the light brown."

Employee: "All right, Mrs. Babcock. We also have the guest towels and washcloths to match. The guest towels are eighty-nine cents. Wouldn't you like six of those also?"

Customer: "Yes, I didn't notice those in the ad. I'm glad you mentioned they are available. Send three guest towels and washcloths in the dark brown and three in the light brown."

Employee: "Thank you, Mrs. Babcock. We also have sheets and pillowcases on sale. What size sheet do you prefer?"

Customer: "The singles—72x108. How much are they?"

Employee: "The singles are $3.49, and you know the regular price is $3.98. The cases are 79 cents for 45x38 size. The regular price is 98 cents. How many would you wish?"

Customer: "You can send six sheets and twelve cases."

Employee: "Will that be enough, Mrs. Babcock?"

Customer: "Yes, thank you."

Employee: "Do you need anything else today?"

Customer: "No, thank you."

Employee: "We'll send these to you, and thank you for your order."

Customer: "Thank you. Good-by."

Employee: "Good-by, Mrs. Babcock."

The customer should hang up the receiver first, not the clerk. The supervisor should have a Telephone Clerk Coaching Memorandum that is completed after every practice call for each clerk. This evaluation sheet enables the supervisor to pinpoint weak-

TELEPHONE CLERK COACHING MEMORANDUM

Clerk_____   Observer_____   Date_____   Time_____

Type of Call	Time Intervals	Total _____
☐ Order	Answering	_____
☐ Mdse. Inquiry	Obtaining Request	_____
☐ Return	Fact Finding	_____
☐ Exchange	Providing Info.	_____
☐ Complaint	Sales Effort	_____
☐ Other	Close	_____

IRREGULARITIES	COMMENTS

Service
___

☐ Improper Announcement
☐ Failed to Get Complete Details
☐ Failed to Report Progress
☐ Unfamiliar with Advr. Mdse.
☐ Called Wrong Dept.
☐ Incomplete or Wrong Info.
☐ Improper Close
☐ Voice Fault
☐ Courtesy Fault

SALES	TYPE	ITEM	AMT.

Sales
___

☐ No Sales Effort Made
☐ Sales Effort Not Appropriate
☐ Item Suggested Not Appropriate
☐ Sales Appeal Not Appropriate
☐ Timing Poor

nesses and correct them. The Telephone Clerk Coaching Memorandum on page 199 is printed here through the courtesy of the Telephone Company.

PLANNING FOR SUGGESTIVE AND MULTIPLE SALES

Based on reports of NRMA (National Retail Merchants Association), various stores, and Telephone Company surveys, here are some of the procedures followed in the planning for suggestive and multiple sales.

A committee of assistant merchandising managers, representing each store division, meets once each week to select the items. They present items from their division as candidates for the next week's telephone selling campaign. No item priced under $2.00 is considered. Preference is given to unadvertised items, or to items not advertised until the week after the telephone campaign. Efforts are also made to provide items that can lead to ensemble and multiple selling. The committee votes on the three best items. These three become the basis for the next week's telephone selling campaign.

In order to help the Telephone Department sell, the committee and buyers meet with the operators. Buyers bring actual samples of merchandise and give detailed information and selling points. Wherever possible, specification sheets are also given to operators. Buyers also give suggestions on "what goes with what," showing operators exactly how ensembles can be built up. Sample ensemble merchandise is left in the Telephone Selling Department as a constant reminder to operators. Operators are instructed to ask for multiple purchases on all applicable merchandise, pointing out convenience and savings to customer. This is especially effective with women's hosiery, pajamas, handkerchiefs, men's and boys' shirts, underwear, sheets, towels, and pillowcases.

DEMONSTRATION HELPS SALES

One store that was surveyed made sure their operators knew all the features on a new washer-dryer just being introduced. They invited the manufacturer's sales representative to give a product demonstration right in the Telephone Selling Department. The sales representative went through a complete demonstration; then answered questions by the group. Specification sheets, highlighting features, were given to all operators. The results were that the Telephone Selling Department sold over one hundred washer-dryers—more than the number sold on the floor.

There is no average figure for telephone sales. A survey conducted by NRMA indicates a range of from 1 to 6 per cent of total store sales being done by telephone. A recent study of fourteen outstanding stores showed a range of from 5 to 14 per cent, with an average of 7 per cent.

HANDLING OF CALLS

Whether you have centralized or decentralized, the handling of calls depends on the volume of the store's telephone sales. Incoming telephone orders can be handled in two ways:

1. Decentralized. Calls are routed from the PBX to the appropriate department for personal attention by a floor clerk. If telephone sales volume is small, floor clerks can handle telephone customers in addition to their in-store customers.

2. Centralized. Telephone sales clerks take all telephone orders and inquiries. When telephone business is sizeable, this method insures the customer prompt attention and enables her to do all her telephone shopping with one call. When necessary, the customer can be connected to the sales floor, with the telephone shopping clerk listening in. The telephone clerk is specially trained and has the necessary reference material and order-taking equipment to handle large volumes of calls in a way that produces *plus* business and creates a favorable "store image" in the eyes of the customer.

With the one-number system, all store calls are answered at the PBX, regardless of their nature. Telephone shopping calls are then routed to the telephone sales department.

With the two-number system—one for store administration, the other for telephone shopping—the telephone customer dials directly to the telephone sales clerk. Where stores actively promote telephone shopping, the trend is toward the two-number system.

SALES ARE LOST WITH DELAYED CALLS

An aggressive telephone shopping department is wasted if customers are *lost* before their calls reach the telephone sales clerks. When customer calls are delayed, sales are lost. The telephone sales clerk answers with identification of the department and her name. The call is personalized immediately.

TWO-NUMBER SYSTEM

With the two-number system, calls go through faster and the traffic load on the main PBX is reduced, reserving these lines for administrative calls. After-hour telephone business can be handled independently of the main PBX, and a separate number lends itself better to promotion of "shopping by telephone." A survey of customers has indicated a preference for the two-number system in telephone shopping departments.

Your telephone company representative can help you decide on facilities best suited to your organization.

CHARGE ACCOUNTS

Whenever a telephone order is sent C.O.D., the operators are trained to suggest that the customer open a charge account. The operators point out the convenience of a charge account. One advantage is that the customer need not remain home to receive the parcel. Other advantages are deferred billing, and no need to carry cash when the customer shops in person.

THE RIGHT MERCHANDISE

As part of a special survey made on telephone shopping, housewives were shown a list of thirty-five representative items of merchandise. They were asked, "Would you worry about ordering these items by telephone?" Here is how the twenty-five items were rated:

High Confidence	Medium Confidence	Low Confidence
Bed linens (highest confidence)	Small electrical appliances	Dining room silverware
Stationery	Table linens	Girdles
Men's underwear	Men's dress shirts	Dining room china and glassware
Children's underwear	Cosmetics	Skirts
Women's hose	Men's sport shirts	Yard goods
Kitchen needs	Bras	Drapes
Toys and games	Curtains	Handbags
Men's socks	Boys' clothing	Costume jewelry
Housedresses	Children's outwear	Women's dresses
Sewing needs	Collars, dickeys, and scarves	Women's shoes
Women's underwear	Women's blouses and sweaters	Women's coats
	Mattresses and springs	Women's hats (lowest confidence)

SUCCESSFUL TELEPHONE SHOPPING DEPARTMENTS

The J. L. Hudson Company, Detroit, Michigan, has one of the largest telephone shopping departments in the United States. Merchandise catalogs and an ad digest eliminate need for a large vertical surface for tear sheets and improve visual supervision. Good design provides space for everything needed by the clerks. Merchandise catalogs and saleschecks are to the left, order turret and dial are to the right, and are angle-mounted for better visibility. The advertising digest is directly in front of the clerk. All surfaces are acoustically treated. A mirror at each position improves tone of service. Screens at the left of the positions flash "out of stock" notices. Conveyor belts operate between each double row of positions.

Stix, Baer, and Fuller, St. Louis, Missouri, has one of the most successful telephone shopping operations in the country. Among the unique features are hinged mounting boards that hold twice as many tear sheets and positive stock control. Saleschecks covering items available in limited quantities are tallied as soon as they come off the conveyor belts. Attendants are required to hold the customer on the line while checking one of the tally clerks for availability of limited-stock merchandise, before completing the sale.

Stix, Baer and Fuller has been experimenting for several years with Automatic Answering Service to record telephone orders after store hours. With the first telephone shopping line connected to the answering device, 3100 calls after hours resulted in $10,-000 sales in a single year, even though the service was not publicized in any manner.

G. L. Freeman, division sales manager of Southern Bell Telephone Company in Miami, said, "From our experience and from many surveys, we find telephone selling brings in profitable business-plus business that supplements, not replaces, in-store sales."

A telephone selling department will increase sales at no increase in inventory and with little capital investment.

HOW THE SECRETARY SHOULD HANDLE TELEPHONE CALLS [1]

Carve each word gently ere you let it fall.
OLIVER WENDELL HOLMES

Life is not so short but that there is always time for courtesy.
RALPH WALDO EMERSON

MOST OF US have mental pigeonholes into which we place people according to their speech. Speech misused can cause considerable discomfort, loss of prestige and business. The woman who speaks, easily and correctly, the standard of speech of the broad language community and business to which she belongs will find herself better off all around. She will be able to make friends and influence people. She will find that her opinions carry greater weight with callers, friends, and business associates. She will be able to express her ideas so as to enhance her value to her employer.

What is the first step in becoming an interesting conversationalist? According to Professor James G. Rogers of Harvard, the first step is "to be able to speak clearly, forcibly, correctly, like gentlefolk." You may possess fascinating depths intellectually and emotionally, but as long as these qualities are hidden in an impenetrable package, they are of no avail. Interesting conversation is the key that can unlock these treasures of personality.

---

[1] Chapter 24 is based on *How to Be a Telephone Belle*, by Mona Ling, 1962, is used by permission of The Dartnell Corporation.

200 MILLION CALLS

Much conversation is face-to-face, while a great deal is accomplished over the telephone voice-to-voice. Today, the telephone is one of the most frequently used means of communication. There are nearly 200 million telephone conversations daily in the United States. More consideration is being given to teaching the role of the telephone in business and social life. Every person who is interested in improvement in the basic communication skills is eager to acquire skill and facility in using the telephone.

When you meet a friend or acquaintance face-to-face, you express cordiality by a smile or a nod. But over the telephone, you must find some other way of transmitting friendliness. What you say and how you say it over the telephone takes the place of the smile or the nod. You can sound confident, courteous, sparkling, and friendly.

WORDS AND MUSIC

William J. Reilly in *Your Life* magazine tells the revealing story of a girl and her reluctant suitor, who sat on a park bench in the moonlight.

"Do you think my eyes are like stars?" she asked him.

He replied, "Yeah."

"And you think my teeth are like pearls?"

"Yeah."

"And you think my hair is like spun gold in the moonlight?"

"Yeah."

"Oh, Joe!" she exclaimed. "You say the most wonderful things!"

Words are put in our mouths for us once in a while, but usually, silent people are relegated to some quiet corner. Even though silent men and women may have virtues, few people have the time to dig them out. If we are to share ideas with others, it is necessary to attain some competence in conversation.

In order to develop an effective telephone technique, keep in mind that your words will be heard, not read. Therefore, you will want to select words that are easily understood by the listener. Words should be short, simple, clear. Avoid complicated words unless some of your conversations with customers or associates require the knowledge and use of a technical vocabulary.

Sentences should be short, simple, clear, with attractive phrases. When you talk, you will realize that you are thinking, and therefore speaking, in ideas. As you express your ideas, you will notice that you distribute the time to pause frequently and naturally. Pausing properly does more than any other thing to make one's conversation natural. It is easy to speak words or sentences, but if you are to receive and give ideas, you must have a depth of understanding and appreciation of communication skills.

MAKE YOUR MESSAGE CLEAR

In all conversation there is danger of making two kinds of mistakes: (1) we give no meaning or a partial meaning; (2) we give the wrong meaning. Make a mental check of past conversations. Have you been asked to repeat sentences or messages? Perhaps you have been giving messages hastily, or your messages are complicated and cannot be clearly understood. Write six or seven messages on a sheet of paper. Check the sentence structure. Are your sentences long, complicated? Is the meaning clear? It is your responsibility to deliver your message so that it is clear to the receiver.

Place your important idea at the beginning of the conversation. If the caller does not understand the idea, clarify it or restate it. Always assume full responsibility immediately if your receiver does not understand the message. Language is the symbol of thought. Language becomes of value only when one person can transmit his thoughts to another person.

PLANNING AND MAKING A CALL

If you are making a business call, you usually have a specific objective: to give or to obtain facts or information. If you are giving information to a customer, here are some suggestions:

1. Make a note of the main idea and subordinate ideas. Have points or ideas arranged in the order of their importance.
2. Have any reference material, reports, lists, ready in case they are needed to complete the call quickly and efficiently.
4. If the call is long-distance, check the time zone for proper time to call. Dial correct number, or place it with the operator.
5. When your customer answers his telephone, identify yourself and your firm, and state the purpose of your call.
6. Give the information to the customer with proper pauses. He then will have an opportunity to take the message correctly and to ask for clarification of any point.
7. If difficult names are given, clarify the spelling by the use of a phonetic alphabet. (See page 211.)
8. Check with the customer to see if he wishes to have any point repeated or clarified; then end the call properly.

ANSWERING CALLS

Answering a business telephone call is very similar to welcoming a visitor. You must convey voice-to-voice the desirable characteristics present in a face-to-face meeting. The caller can only judge the reception and gain an impression by what he hears. Therefore, the attainment of accuracy, skill, and courtesy by business people can become a source of profit for the firm.

In answering calls, you have specific objectives to accomplish. These objectives impose certain responsibilities on you. When you answer the telephone, you represent the boss and the firm.

1. Give the caller the impression that his call is a welcome one, and that you are interested in him and his requests.
2. Give the caller the impression that his call will be handled satisfactorily and efficiently.
3. Listen to the caller without interrupting him until he makes the purpose of his call known.
4. Use the caller's name frequently but not obviously, and take care of his request as quickly as possible.
5. Let him know what you are doing. If you have to leave your desk for a moment to obtain information, let him know. If you are transferring the call to another department or executive, let the caller know.

6. If your caller wants to talk to the boss, let him know that the call is going through or that the boss is talking on another line.
7. If the boss is not available or you cannot put the call through to him, offer to be of assistance or to take a message.
8. Be prepared to take a message at all times. If you take a message and end the conversation, let the caller hang up first, if at all possible.

ANNOUNCING IDENTIFICATION

Every telephone should be answered with proper identification of the firm, the department or the office. With the exception of the switchboard operator, every person should identify herself after identification of the department, office, desk or station.

"Mr. Johnson's office; Miss Hall."
"Dr. Brown's office; Miss Whitaker."
"Ace Construction Company; Mrs. Jones."
"Adjustment Department; Miss Green."

WHAT TO SAY WHEN

The Called Party Is Not Available

"Mr. Johnson is talking on another telephone. May I help you?"

"I'm sorry, Mr. Lewis, but Mr. Douglas is talking on another telephone. Do you wish to wait, or may he call you?"

"I'm sorry, Mr. Swift is in another office. I expect him back at 10:00 o'clock. May I tell him who called?"

"Mr. Potter is talking on another telephone. If I may have your name and telephone number, I will ask him to call you as soon as he can."

Offering to Assist the Caller

"Mr. Clark will be on vacation until the first of the month. May I help you?"

"Mr. Gilbert will be out of town until Tuesday. May I help you?"

"Mr. Grant is out of the office. I expect him back tomorrow morning. May I help you?"

"Mr. Wilson is on vacation. However, his assistant, Mr. Curtis, is here. Would you like to talk with him?"

"I'm sorry, but Mr. Thompson is out of the city this week. May I help you or give him a message?"

Transferring a Call

"I'm sorry, but you have reached the wrong extension. May I transfer you to the correct extension?"

"I'm sorry, but Mr. Drake is out of the city. However, Mr. Richards is taking his calls. May I transfer you to Mr. Richards' office?"

"I'm sorry, but Mr. White had to leave the office before your call. He asked me to tell you that Mr. Doe has the information you want."

Interrupting the Call

"It will take a minute to get that information from Mr. Hart's office. Do you care to wait, or may I call you back with the information?"

"I have the report ready for you, Mr. Williams. Will you excuse me while I get it?" (Upon returning to the telephone say, "Thank you for waiting, Mr. Williams.")

TAKING A MESSAGE

Taking a message for the boss or another executive or employee should be relatively simple. However, a great deal of business is lost each year by incomplete or "forgotten" messages. A courteous person returns telephone calls. Accurate messages reduce errors and eliminate unnecessary calls.

When I was in Miami, Florida, Mrs. Sally Gould, of the public relations department of Southern Bell Telephone Company, invited me to visit her office. We were exchanging ideas on telephone communication, when the subject of taking messages was mentioned. Mrs. Gould listed several points that she uses in training business personnel and in taking her own messages. (Her messages are so complete that they are filed as a permanent reference.)

What To Record	*The Reason Why*
TO WHOM—Name of person called.	To insure delivery to the proper person.
FROM WHOM—Name of the caller and his business connection.	There may be persons of similar names in different businesses.
WHERE—Caller's telephone number and extension number.	May be impossible to call back without total information.

WHERE—Caller's city and state (if long-distance).

Similar exchange names and telephone numbers may be repeated in many of the states.

WHAT—Message itself.

Self-evident.

WHY—Action requested and the action promised.

To assure fulfillment of any commitments.

HOW—Under certain circumstances, the number of the long-distance operator handling the call.

To facilitate reestablishing the call at a later time.

BY WHOM—Names of the person who recorded the message.

In case clarifying questions should be asked.

WHEN—Date and hour of the call.

On occasion, the time of the call may be as essential as the message itself.

To assure the accuracy and completeness of a message, you might consider the following suggestions:

1. Listen attentively to the message.
2. Record the message while it is being given.
3. Check to be sure all telephone numbers are correct.
4. Verify the spelling of difficult names, using a phonetic alphabet. (See below.)
5. After the telephone call has been completed, make additional notes from memory, if necessary.
6. Attach to the message any papers, reports, lists of information that would be helpful to the called party.

PHONETIC ALPHABET

Here is the phonetic alphabet used by the United States Government in the verification of spelling of difficult names:

A as in ALFA

B as in BRAVO

C as in CHARLIE

D as in DELTA

E as in ECHO

F as in FOX TROT

G as in GOLF

H as in HOTEL

I as in INDIA

J as in JULIET

K as in KILO

L as in LIMA

M as in MIKE
N as in NOVEMBER
O as in OSCAR
P as in PAPA
Q as in QUEBEC
R as in ROMEO
S as in SIERRA

T as in TANGO
U as in UNIFORM
V as in VICTOR
W as in WHISKEY
X as in X-RAY
Y as in YANKEE
Z as in ZULU

In verifying names, it often is not enough to merely spell the name, since some letters like *P* and *B*, *T* and *D*, *F* and *S*, are frequently confused. It is possible to say, "Is that *B* as in 'BRAVO,' or *P* as in 'PAPA'?"

You should have definite words to use in the spelling of difficult names. Otherwise, you will be mentally trying to think of a name and will forget the message.

TESTED TIPS

The ten tips on telephone technique listed below were sent to me by Alice King Snavely, secretary to Stanley Marcus of Neiman-Marcus in Dallas, Texas:

OUT?	Never during store hours. Your customer expects your attention. Few things are more irritating than the telephone that rings and rings, with no answer.
RULE ONE	There must be someone to answer your telephone when you are away.
QUICKLY	Pick up the receiver before your customer gets impatient. Nobody likes being ignored.
RULE TWO	Answer your telephone immediately.
READY?	You're on the air. Your customer needs help. You may be asked for information or to take a message. Your rating slips if you are cut off while searching for equipment.
RULE THREE	Always have a pencil, note pad, and reference materials by the telephone.
WHO?	"Hello" is an answer; but why not give your station identification?

RULE FOUR	Answer by giving your department and your name.
NAME	"Yes, sir" is adequate, but "Yes, Mr. Cook" will cause your customer to perk up his ears. Everyone enjoys the sound of his own name.
RULE FIVE	Address your customers by name whenever possible.
STATIC	Unpleasant distractions are gum-chewing, background conversation, or giggles.
RULE SIX	Be ready to talk when you pick up the receiver. Speak distinctly, pleasantly, and naturally.
SILENCE	Silence is not always golden. It can make your customer feel like the forgotten man.
RULE SEVEN	Explain any necessary delays in the conversation. Leave the line for as brief a period as possible.
WATCH	Rapid, drawled, whispered, or shouted speech will make your conversation less effective.
RULE EIGHT	Speak directly into the mouthpiece with your lips about one-half inch away. Keep your speech clear and distinct.
MUSIC	Yes, it's music to hear "please" and "thank you" regularly.
RULE NINE	Be tactful in your choice of words. Make "please" a regular in your telephone vocabulary.
TONE	It's not always *what* you say; often, it's *how* you say it.
RULE TEN	Be interested; sound interested.

YOUR VOICE IS YOU

When you use the telephone, your voice is you, your firm or organization. In every business telephone conversation, you represent or misrepresent your boss or firm or both. The impressions your voice makes on the telephone may influence the customer to stop doing business or to continue doing business with your firm.

More than $50 million is lost annually in the United States because of the way business telephone operators, personnel, secretaries, and executives use the telephone. In many cases, this business was placed at considerable expense and effort on the part of many persons. But this business can be lost within sixty to ninety seconds through one discourteous telephone call.

HOW A MILLION WAS LOST

A recent telephone call set a record for a business loss. The representative of a firm had spent several months to obtain a con-

---

TEST YOURSELF

Effective Telephone Service

	Yes	No	Some-times
1. Do I answer my telephone on the first ring?	____	____	____
2. Do I transact business quickly, thus keeping the telephone more available for incoming customer calls?	____	____	____
3. Do I have frequently requested information available near the telephone?	____	____	____
4. Do I make arrangements for my telephone to be answered when I am away?	____	____	____
5. Do I give the customer the choice of waiting (while information is obtained) or of being called back?	____	____	____
6. Do I make a sincere effort to help the customer with the information desired?	____	____	____
7. Were opportunities for future business developed?	____	____	____
8. If the customer had a complaint, was he given a full opportunity to express himself?	____	____	____
9. Do I indicate a willingness to be of service, in my voice and manner?	____	____	____
10. Was a definite and mutually satisfactory arrangement decided?	____	____	____

For every YES answer, add ten points.
For every SOMETIMES answer, add two points.

100 points   —Perfect score
80-90 points   —Excellent rating
70 points   —Satisfactory rating
Below 70 points—Attention to improvement in attitude
　　　　　　　　　and service is needed.

tract with a potential customer. The customer telephoned one of the representatives to place the business with his firm. While attempting to get the representative on the telephone, the customer was insulted by a rude, untrained, inconsiderate switchboard operator, and the call was ended at the switchboard. The loss was a million dollars in business. It had taken several months to obtain the contract and one minute to lose it.

Your voice should convey by telephone what you would ordinarily express face-to-face by gestures, visible expressions, or a smile. A smile will transmit a warm, friendly personality over the wire. A dour expression will transmit the image of an unpleasant "Miss Grim" over the telephone.

There are many ways to say one simple sentence. The tone of voice can convey different meanings for each sentence, though the words may be the same. Here are some of the types who lose business for their employers and their firms. Unfortunately, these "personalities" misrepresent their firms:

Miss Discourtesy: "I can't give the call to him until I know who's calling." (Speaks in a high-pitched tone of voice that expresses annoyance, impatience, frustration, and possibly anger.)

Miss Disgusted: "I didn't have anything to do with your shipment. I just work here." (Speaks in low, flat, colorless voice, with complete disinterest in the caller.)

Miss Arrogance: "He's busy. You'll have to wait a minute." (Angrily) "I said you'll have to wait a minute." (Speaks with domineering tone; treats every caller as if he were an intruder.)

Miss Weary: "I don't know whether he is in or not. Some of the people aren't at their desks yet. It's kinda early—why don't you call back?" (Speaks wearily, with a tired voice; lacks color, emotion, vitality, energy.)

Miss Gush: "Good morning! ABC Company; Miss Gush speaking. May I be of service to you?" (She bubbles over with eagerness to do too much and say too much. She overtalks, interrupts, and lacks emotional and vocal control.)

Miss Sarcastic: "Well, what do you want me to do about it? That's the company's rule. I didn't make it." (Her acid tones imply, "Why don't you drop dead?" She is poison to a boss or to a firm.)

Miss Breathless: "XYZ Company (*puff-puff*); Miss Breathless (*puff-puff*) speaking." (Her voice sounds as though she had run up ten flights of stairs to answer the phone. Her sentences are choppy, disconnected; she lacks poise, breath control, assurance; needs proper voice work.)

Miss Authority: "Look, I've been here thirteen years and I don't care what the boss says, we don't have that item and we've never had it." (Throws her weight around like a bomb. Explodes when her authority is questioned. She is decisive—right or wrong; interrupts the caller; doesn't listen. She has a distorted mental image of what the word *authority* means.)

Miss Indecisive: "Well-uh, I've heard someone mention that, but I don't quite remember what it was all about. Uh—I really don't know what to tell you. Perhaps—uh— why don't you check with the operator? She's been here a long time," (Answers telephone and conducts conversations with doubt and uncertainty. Is unsure of herself; can't make decisions or handle calls effectively.)

Miss Impatience: "You've got to speak louder if you want me to help you. Did you say 'Dunn'? Is that *D* as in 'Dunce'?" (Voice and manner are discourteous. Sentences are sharp, abrupt. Interrupts caller; places all responsibility for "not hearing" on him. She is rude, inconsiderate, and irritable.)

COURTESY COUNTS

Lucille Hurst, secretary to T. E. Manwarring, branch manager of Owens-Illinois in Los Angeles, California, believes that courtesy is extremely important in every telephone conversation. When answering Mr. Manwarring's telephone, Lucille follows these procedures:

Identification	"Mr. Manwarring's office, Miss Hurst."
Not available	"I'm sorry, but Mr. Manwarring is out of town. I expect him to return Thursday. May I help you?"

or "Mr. Manwarring is out to lunch. I expect him back at 1:30. May I have him call you when he returns?"

or "I'm sorry, but Mr. Manwarring is out of the office. May I help you or give him a message?"

Asking caller to wait "Mr. Manwarring is talking on another telephone. Do you wish to wait, or may he telephone you?"

Lucille identifies her office and herself immediately with a friendly voice and manner. She listens attentively to the caller, offers to help or take a message. In taking a message, she verifies spelling, addresses, telephone numbers, and any other pertinent information. When a call is ended, she waits for the caller to hang up first.

SCREENING CALLS

Today, many executives answer their own telephones. They feel that this personalizes calls, which it does. It also reduces errors, increases efficiency in handling calls, and saves valuable time for the executive and his secretary. However, some executives are engaged in many different activities over a vast area, which makes it impossible for them to handle their telephone calls. Their calls must be screened, so that general information requests can be handled by their staffs. It takes a tactful, courteous, efficient woman to screen calls, handle them, and leave the caller with the feeling that he has received personal service.

One secretary who does an excellent public relations job for her boss is Virginia Roberts, assistant secretary to John L. Bodette, general manager of the Florists' Telegraph Delivery Association, at international headquarters in Detroit, Michigan.

Virginia and the other two secretaries answer their phones on the first ring. Virginia answers, "Miss Roberts," as she receives many telephone calls requesting general information. However, the other two secretaries answer, "Mr. Bodette's office"; then identify themselves.

After identification, a tactful inquiry is made as to the name of the caller and another as to the nature of the call, if this information is not volunteered. If a secretary can handle the request, the call is ended at that point. If the caller wishes to discuss some matter with Mr. Bodette, the call is announced to him. If the call pertains to specific information in the file, that file is given to Mr. Bodette before the call proceeds very far.

In taking messages, the three secretaries keep a complete day-to-day telephone log of all incoming calls, regardless of the disposition of them. This log consists of the name of the caller, the date and time, the disposition of the call, and the initials of the person taking the call. This eliminates the possibility of an error or a "forgotten" message and gives a thorough checkback on persons who have called.

WELL-INFORMED ASSISTANT

During the years that I lived in California, it was necessary to make frequent calls to the University of California Extension for information. It soon became a habit to telephone Mrs. Virginia Gandy, as she had the information or knew where to obtain it.

Virginia is the administrative assistant to Dr. Robert B. Haas, head of arts and humanities, University Extension, UCLA. She attended UCLA and did graduate work at the University of California in Berkeley. Therefore, Virginia has a good background in the department and the University Extension. She keeps well informed on all the workings in the various areas, so that she can quickly take care of most of the calls for general information. Here is how she handles calls:

Identification	"Dr. Haas' office; Mrs. Gandy."
Not available	"May I take a message for Dr. Haas?"
or	"May I have Dr. Haas telephone you?"
Keeping caller *Waiting on phone*	"Yes, Dr. Haas is in, but he's talking on another line. Do you wish to wait, or may I have him call you?"
Caller waiting	"Yes, may I tell Dr. Haas who's calling, please?" (Pause for name.) "Thank you, Mr. Smith. He should be through in a few moments." (Virginia leaves the line, gives Dr. Haas a complete memo on the call now waiting.)
Thirty seconds later	"Hello, Mr. Smith." (Obtains caller's attention gently.) "I'm sorry; Dr. Haas is still talking. He shouldn't be on his line much longer. Do you wish to wait, or may I have him call you?"
Twenty seconds later	Dr. Haas answers the call with an apology for keeping the caller waiting.

It is very important in a university to have proper titles before returning calls. Therefore, Virginia tries to keep informed as to the titles of the callers and obtains that information from persons with whom she is not familiar. Complete information is taken on the caller's name and title, nature of call, time of day, and the specific message. Many of the messages require additional information—a paper, report, list, written information on classes, or biographical data that will speed up Dr. Haas' return calls. The proper information is attached to each message. The messages are placed on Dr. Haas' desk in the order of their official importance; are then kept for a permanent file and for future reference.

Virginia keeps Dr. Haas informed about all calls that she has taken for him, so that he will know the background if he receives a call from the same person. She keeps herself informed on calls that he makes, so that in his absence she can answer intelligently if the same person calls again.

PLEASANT CONVERSATIONS

> *Conversation is an art in which a man has all mankind for competitors.*
>
> EMERSON

It is estimated that 90 per cent of all communication is oral. Conversation is the great universal need of mankind. Have you ever stopped to think what would happen if you could not transmit your thoughts to others? Or what would happen if others could not share their ideas and experiences with you? Without language most human activity would cease.

Language is a living thing. It is a symbol of thought. As our skills in conversation grow and develop, our lives become enriched. Our happiness depends to a great extent upon our ability to communicate with others. Our success depends to a great degree upon our ability to perfect telephone techniques in business communication.

It is most important to acquire skills and techniques in a subject. However, a knowledge of skills and techniques will not make improvement possible until they become a part of our thoughts, emotions, attitudes, and experiences. The mind conceives the thought, the imagination visualizes the situation, and emotion is expressed in our voice. Emotion affects the quality of the voice. We evoke favorable responses from others through the emotion expressed in our voice. We stimulate others in the degree that we are interested.

While reading Virginia Roberts' letter on her telephone procedures, I saw a quotation printed on the Florists' Telegraph Delivery Association stationery. It read: "Something warm and human and understanding happens when you send flowers by wire."

How much more pleasant life would be if everyone realized that "Something warm and human and understanding happens when people engage in pleasant conversations."

TEST YOURSELF

	Yes	No	Some-times
1. Do you know what you are going to say on the telephone?	___	___	___
2. Is it easy for you to begin a telephone conversation?	___	___	___
3. Do you easily find words to express yourself in telephone conversations?	___	___	___
4. Do you avoid using slang and trite phrases?	___	___	___
5. Do you listen without interrupting?	___	___	___
6. Do you avoid exaggerating?	___	___	___
7. Do you smile while talking on the telephone?	___	___	___
8. Do you avoid long conversations on the telephone?	___	___	___
9. Do you use your caller's name frequently?	___	___	___
10. Can you end the conversation without being abrupt?	___	___	___
11. Do people easily understand you on the telephone?	___	___	___
12. Are you interested in what you are going to say on the telephone?	___	___	___
13. Do you feel that others are interested in what you say?	___	___	___
14. Are you quick to discover the purpose of your customer's call?	___	___	___
15. Do you visualize your caller as being near you?	___	___	___
16. Do you find it easy to handle difficult people over the telephone?	___	___	___
17. Do you refrain from reprimanding over the telephone a person who has done something to displease you?	___	___	___
18. Do you refrain from grumbling over the telephone about things you cannot change?	___	___	___
19. Do you refrain from trying to impress those with whom you talk on the telephone?	___	___	___
20. Do you refrain from discussing other people's business on the telephone?	___	___	___

21. Do you look forward to telephone conversations?   ____ ____ ____
22. Do you feel comfortable conversing with anyone regardless of age or position?   ____ ____ ____
23. Do you find it easy to remember names of frequent callers?   ____ ____ ____
24. Do you speak in a pleasant tone, despite pressures and upsets?   ____ ____ ____
25. Do you conduct yourself in a professional manner over the telephone?   ____ ____ ____

For every YES answer, add 4 points.
For every SOMETIMES answer, add 1 point.

100 points   —Perfect score
80-90 points   —Excellent rating
70 points   —Satisfactory rating
Below 70 points—Start on a self-improvement program immediately, with special emphasis on telephone technique.

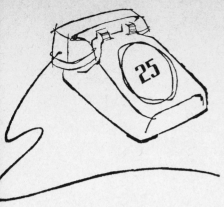

DEVELOPMENT
OF LISTENING SKILLS

Silence and reserve suggest latent power. What some men think has more effect than what others say.

CHESTERFIELD

IT IS ESTIMATED that 90 per cent of all communication is oral. In every conversation there is a listener, yet we pay the least attention to listening. Though it is the communication skill most often used, listening is the weakest of the four basic communication skills. Somehow we have managed to acquire some skills in writing, speaking, and reading. But, for the most part, we have managed to escape development of our skills in listening.

Recently when I was training some companies in Dallas, I went into a letter shop near my hotel. A sign on the desk intrigued me. The sign said, "Don't talk while I'm interrupting." For some strange reason, salemen prefer to talk to their prospects rather than to listen to them. If the prospect attempts to talk, the salesman interrupts and expresses his views. He loses the appointment in many cases. He believes that he did not have a *good prospect*, but actually the prospect just didn't have a *good listener*.

INTERRUPTING THE PROSPECT

A salesman who has developed listening skills will not interrupt his prospect over the telephone, unless it is absolutely necessary to do so. If interrupted, the prospect will frequently become annoyed, irritated, or frustrated and will end the conversation abruptly. The prospect has been, temporarily at least, deprived of his freedom of speech. He had something to say and it was important to him, if not to the salesman.

Here are a few well-known "killers" of interviews:[1]

1. Inserting your own "pet" word or phrase, if the prospect hesitates for a moment.
2. Finishing the prospect's sentence for him. You are finishing his sentence at your own pre-established habit of thinking, which is completely different from the prospect's habit of thinking.
3. Attempting to rush a prospect who speaks slowly. The rate of speech has nothing to do with the prospect's intelligence. He has become conditioned to speaking slowly and won't change his habit of speech to do business with you.
4. Lacking clarity in your expression. More interviews have been lost because the prospect did not know what the caller wanted him to do than for any other reason. Lack of clarity invites irritating questions from the prospect to find out "what the call is about." These questions sometimes affect the caller.
5. Showing impatience at requests for additional information, or in answering questions, or in overcoming objections.
6. Educating your prospect over the telephone, which invites questions that cannot be answered at the point of the telephone. Educating the prospect over the telephone almost always ends in the salesman doing all of the talking and the prospect doing all of the listening.
7. Talking while the prospect is talking. You might win this "battle of words" but you will lose the appointment.
8. Failing to listen to the indicators of attention and interest. Listening will enable you to observe these indicators and to use them to your greatest advantage in obtaining the interview and in closing the sale during the sales interview.
9. Estimating inaccurately the degree of emotional involvement and suggestibility of the prospect.
10. Projecting your own opinions, fears, insecurities, or thinking out to the prospect. One of the first determining factors in effective telephoning is to learn self-discipline and control. A salesman's thoughts, feelings, fears, insecurities may be transmitted over the telephone and evoke the wrong kind of response from the prospect. A salesman's prejudices and strong opinions will affect his listening skills and will lose appointments.

---

[1] Reprinted through permission of *Specialty Salesman*, October 1962.

SUCCESSFUL TELEPHONE SALESMAN

"While they talk, I listen and sell." [2] This statement was made by Howard J. Richard, C.L.U., insurance salesman extraordinary, who sells over $5 million of life insurance a year, excluding pension plans and group insurance. Howard says that he owes his success to that wonderful instrument, the telephone, and to his skill in listening.

From the day he joined New York Life Insurance Company in 1935 until he entered the U. S. Army in 1942, Howard Richard was moderately successful. Being in the service gave him a chance to make an objective analysis of his prospecting methods. He decided that he had wasted time and energy in going from place to place, waiting to see prospective clients. He had also wasted time seeing unproductive people. He estimated that he could reach ten times as many persons in a day through the effective use of the telephone.

Howard discovered that selling over the telephone was twice as difficult as selling in person, but he could reach ten times as many persons in a day. The result was five times as many sales. His first year back from service saw Howard reaching the million-dollar sales mark. His sales have continued to soar. For the past several years, he has been his company's top producer in individual sales for New England and New York.

Howard Richard knows that a good listener can "listen" himself into more appointments or sales than a poor listener can obtain by talking. He knows, too, there is no communication until the message is received, so he encourages the prospect to talk. He asks questions that provoke answers he can use to his advantage in "problem-solving." As the salesman's purpose is to persuade, Howard leans heavily upon questions, suggestions, and motivational statements that evoke favorable responses in his prospects. But for the most part, he listens to his customers.

Howard believes the prospect must share in the responsibility of understanding the message; therefore, his delivery is clear, concise, and sincere. He arranges his material so those who hear

---

[2] Reprinted through the courtesy of *Insurance Salesman*, May 1962.

him agree with his ideas and are influenced by his suggestions. He speaks with warmth, interest, and sincerity. He is the complete opposite of the high-pressure, hard-selling insurance agent. His patience and courtesy are qualities that help in telephoning. His sense of security is strong enough that he can afford to be silent and let the prospect talk. The greatest control that a salesman can have over his prospect is the mental capacity to listen attentively and accurately, with the ability to exercise good judgment in the use of the prospect's information.

DIFFICULTIES IN LISTENING

Many more sound waves enter our ears than we wish to hear, so we have learned to shut out most of the extraneous ones. We can ignore many of the sounds that are impinging on our ears. By concentrating on our present activity, we withdraw ourselves from those sounds that do not contribute to the success of our activity. We should control our telephoning environment to enable us to concentrate more fully on the conversations and on what the prospect is saying.

But often our difficulty in listening is within us. Here are a few of the many reasons why we don't listen to prospects:

FEARS AND INSECURITIES

Many salesmen have a fear of talking on the phone to an unseen audience. They build up psychological barriers before they dial a telephone number. Both the salesman and the prospect are affected by these psychological barriers. The caller's emotional state, fears, insecurities, affect the message and the response of the receiver. When we have fears and insecurities in telephoning, our sense of insecurity makes us want to dominate the conversation. If we dominate the conversation, we cannot listen to the prospect. If we do not listen to the prospect, we cannot determine what he is saying or how he likes to be treated as a person. Skill is needed to draw the prospect out and to find out how he thinks and acts. Skill is needed to find out how the prospect is most comfortable as a person and how he likes to be considered in the eyes of other people.

FEELINGS OF NEGATIVITY AND ANTAGONISM

Many salesmen permit their feelings of negativity and personal antagonism to interfere with listening. Many persons feel negative about making a telephone call before they dial a number. Some men *know* in advance that the prospect will be rude, unfriendly, will resist their idea, will object to their request for an interview. When these salesmen reach the prospect, this negativity is transmitted over the wire in thoughts, feelings, emotions, and voice. This negativity affects the salesman's ability to listen and the receiver's response to the call. The salesman believes the prospect's statements or questions are negative and are in conflict with his own ideas and basic concepts. The salesman jumps to his own defense mentally, if not verbally.

As the salesman's purpose is to persuade the prospect to listen to an idea and to grant an interview, he must establish a friendly atmosphere at the outset. He must use psychological devices of suggestion and motivation in order to establish a positive response. He must express sincerity, warmth, and interest in order to establish the rapport necessary to obtain an appointment. The feelings of negativism and antagonism set up the opposite response in the prospect, and he reacts negatively to any idea or suggestion of the salesman.

INABILITY TO LISTEN TO TOTAL MEANING

Many salesmen listen to the words of the prospect without listening for the message. Many salesmen read an approach to a prospect, the prospect objects, then the salesman reads an answer that is applicable to that objection from a list of "answers to common objections." The prospect is not satisfied with the answer and gives another objection.

The prospect is giving the salesman two messages when he asks questions, makes statements, or gives objections. The prospect is giving: (1) the content of the message, and (2) the feeling underlying this content. The feeling of one prospect will, in most cases, be different from the feeling of other prospects, though the content may be the same.

For example, one prospect might say, "I *can't afford* to buy anything." Another prospect might say, "I can't afford *to buy anything*." The content is the same, yet the feelings of both prospects are different. This difference can be detected in the voice, manner, intonation, inflection, emotional color, emphasis, and feeling.

In my training programs for small groups of participants, I ask the group to divide into two groups and stand facing each other. One group will assume the role of the prospect; the other will assume the role of the salesman. As each prospect objects, the salesman translates the meaning of the objection both by *content* and *feeling*. These translations of the group are determined by the prospect's words, voice, manner, personality, and feeling that is transmitted to the salesman. Within a short period of time the entire group will become more sensitive to listening and will be able to overcome any objection more effectively.

LACK OF INTEREST IN PROSPECT

Psychologists say that we spend most of the time thinking about ourselves. It requires discipline and training to think of the other person—his needs, wishes, problems, desires—and to speak to him with a "customer-you" attitude. Also, for some strange reason, many salesmen feel that their knowledge is superior to that of the prospect. This superiority is indicated in their tone of voice and manner. The salesman who is extremely egocentric is usually in love with the sound of his own voice. He treats the prospect's remarks as mere interruptions and believes that his contribution to the conversation is more worthwhile than that of the prospect.

Many prospects can detect *faked* interest or *lack* of interest. The prospect wants the salesman to *be* interested in him. During his entire life, the prospect has been learning to think of himself in certain ways. He has built up images of himself. He is aware of many of his needs, wants, desires, comforts, and is interested in knowing how the salesman can help him satisfy these drives or needs. He wants to know: "What can you do for me?" "How can you help me to get what I want?"

The successful salesman gives the impression that he is genuinely interested in the prospect, and he is. Mentally, he says, "I'm interested in you as a person, in what you say and do, in how you think and feel. I'm interested in being of service to you." The successful salesman knows that genuine interest will get results.

MENTAL LAZINESS

Many salesmen have low, vague goals. They are completely disorganized and work on a hit-or-miss basis. They do not have any specific work patterns. These persons will not put forth the mental effort required to listen to the prospect. They merely "wait out" the prospect's remarks, then start talking again. They are not mentally alert in handling prospects or in overcoming objections. The mind of a disorganized, inefficient salesman is somewhat like a restless wanderer, who flits here and there and everywhere and doesn't stop anywhere long enough to accomplish anything worthwhile. He cannot concentrate on what the prospect is saying long enough to translate the message. He has the ability to be mentally alert but not the desire. Without desire, nothing can be accomplished.

LACK OF PREPARATION

The salesman who attempts to telephone without preparing his presentation will find it difficult to listen to the prospect. He will be busy trying to think of something to say, while the prospect is

talking. In most cases, he will not hear all of the objection; therefore, he cannot overcome it effectively. If the prospect is not
satisfied with the answer, he will give another objection.

The reaction of most unprepared salesmen is usually one of the
following: (1) he will attempt to overcome the objection stated,
and if unsuccessful, will hang up; or (2) he will fumble, hesitate,
or stammer and lose the appointment; or (3) he will become
nervous and race along with rambling sentences that really don't
say anything or do anything. An unprepared salesman lacks poise,
confidence, and technique.

Dr. G. Herbert True, lecturer and special consultant to many
business firms said, "The less you know about a subject, the more
you talk." For the most part, the more you talk in a telephone
conversation without really saying anything, the greater are your
chances of losing the appointment.

LACK OF MATURITY

We cannot employ effective listening techniques if our attitudes
are in conflict with what we are doing. We cannot say one thing
while believing another and hope to win a favorable response, unless we have trained ourselves to act in this way. The immature
salesman feels that his position is being jeopardized if the prospect
asks questions or objects to his request for an interview. He is on
the defensive. He expects criticism, rudeness, hostility, and anger.
The prospect might ask questions, make statements, or give objections in an attempt to clarify the idea or to gain more information. The mature salesman does not resent these questions,
statements, or objections. He is prepared to handle them smoothly,
efficiently, with persuasive tones that evoke favorable responses.

The mature salesman thinks of the prospect, his needs, desires,
wants, and how he wants to be treated as a person. He adopts a
"customer-you" attitude. He learns to express himself in language
the prospect can understand. When this message is received, it
becomes a stimulus for action.

We cannot perform our job satisfactorily if we are emotionally involved with our own wishes, needs, wants, desires, problems, and cannot set them aside to think of another person. The process of listening involves the whole person. The process of listening actively involves maturity within that person.

LACK OF TECHNIQUE

There are limits to the effectiveness of do-it-yourself methods. The salesman who has not learned a technique of getting appointments has not learned to listen carefully to the prospect. Without technique, the salesman lacks the control of himself and of the prospect. This lack of control will make it impossible for him to listen as effectively as he can with technique and control.

A salesman should study the basic rules of telephoning and communication skills in order to achieve success in obtaining appointments. The type of technique you should develop is the one that has the widest acceptance and has the greatest potential in insuring your success. Once a technique is gained and can be put to work for you, it can help you in your business or social life. This preparation will enable you to further develop your communication skills, particularly that of listening.

LACK OF FEEDBACK MECHANISM

Some salesmen can give a mechanical approach without any creativity or imagination and can get some appointments. However, they cannot follow through effectively when the prospect makes a statement or asks a question or gives an objection. Every person who uses the telephone should learn how to listen to the prospect's words, phrases, vocabulary, message, voice, rate of speech, nuances of emotion and thought, and to indicators of interest. He should learn how to adapt, change, modify, and use this information to obtain an appointment. The salesman must acquire some degree of skill in listening in order to develop a "feedback" mechanism.

A machine that employs a "feedback" mechanism does not complete an operation in a rigid, unalterable way but has, within itself, devices for gathering information about the process, according to the information that it collects. "Feedback" is a basic characteristic of the cybernetic mechanism. It designates the feeding back of information to the machine during a process that enables the machine to adjust itself to changing conditions.

The salesman is, or ought to be, a "feedback" mechanism. He ought to have the capacity to listen accurately to information, gather it, adjust to it quickly, and adapt it for his own use. It is highly improbable that a salesman can achieve great success in telephoning or in selling until he develops this "feedback" principle. Development of this "feedback" through effective listening also enables the salesman to increase sales. There is a definite relationship between *listening* and *closing*, whether it is used at the point of the telephone or in the field.

CLOSE SALE ON TELEPHONE

In working with many salesmen on their communication problems, it has been my observation that a man who increases his skill in listening is better able to establish a friendly relationship with the prospect. He is able to command attention, control the interview (through listening, not talking), overcome objections, and obtain appointments. It has also been my observation that this man can increase his ratio of appointments to calls, and sales to interviews, within a short period of time. Depending upon his abilities and objectives, he can also close the sale on the telephone, if he wishes to do so. Naturally, this depends, too, on the product or service.

Howard Richard says, "The biggest difference between mediocrity and success is the salesman's skill in using the telephone for prospecting and closing sales."

Howard believes that the experienced salesman who is proficient in the use of the telephone can make the sale over the telephone. He does not believe in telling the prospect much of anything. Howard would much rather listen to the prospect develop his own story in response to the appropriate question from him.

For example, almost without exception, Howard's opening approach is:

"My name is Howard Richard. I represent the New York Life Insurance Company in the Greater Boston area, and I just called to find out what you have been doing about life insurance up to now, if you care to tell me." [3]

Howard identifies himself and his company and states his purpose immediately. He brings up specific information that he has learned about the prospect. He is prepared before he dials the number. He is clear, concise, low-pressure, with good vocal delivery. As a telephone approach appeals solely to the ear, Howard knows the sound of the voice and the appeal of the approach will, to a great extent, determine the success of the call.

Howard says, "If you flop just once in a telephone conversation, you're all done." Howard doesn't flop in his telephone calls, because he sells a policy a day, ranging in size from $10,000 to $30,000, with an average total of three hundred individual sales each year. Skills in telephoning and in listening keep Howard's production where it is. The difference between mediocrity and success is the salesman's skill in using the telephone and in the development of his communication skills, particularly listening.

---

[3] Reprinted through the courtesy of *Insurance Salesman*, May 1962.

HOW TO IMPROVE
YOUR SPEECH

*Good talk is like scenery—continuous, yet constantly varying,
and full of the charm of novelty and surprise.*

RANDOLPH S. BOURNE

WHEREVER YOU ARE, no matter what your station in
life may be, you cannot do without speech. Every speech, every
conversation, whether the audience is large or small, has as its
goal the gaining of a response. When someone speaks to you,
that someone is trying to gain a certain response from you. When
you speak to another person, you are asking for a response from
that individual.

WHAT IS EFFECTIVE SPEECH?

Effective speech has been defined as bigger and better conversation. Also, effective speech is the most direct utterance suited
to the audience and the occasion. Effective speech includes sharing
ideas, feelings, moods, and information.

It sounds strange to say that effective speech includes more
than speaking correctly. The nonverbal levels of communication
are very much a part of effective speech. Nonverbal communication includes those ways in which we communicate without using

234

words. For example, eye contact or looking people in the eye when speaking is a nonverbal way of communication. A salesman or manager might shake his fist in indignation or pound his desk to make a point. Nonverbal communication also includes distracting habits, like rattling change in the pocket, constant hair pulling, scratching, twisting a ring, looking at a wrist watch too often, and continual adjustment of the glasses. For the most effective speech performance, nonverbal and verbal levels of speaking must be coordinated in an attractive manner.

THE MIRROR—YOUR SPEECH TEACHER

Presuming you are not going to avail yourself of a speech teacher, your mirror is your next best teacher. So start talking to yourself in the mirror, and observe. Try not to change the general manner in which you usually speak. During this process and with the exercises and practice following, it may prove soothing for you to have the background music of your radio or record player. This relaxing music tends to make you concentrate more closely on what you are doing. You listen more carefully to yourself rather than to the music, and, generally speaking, it makes you less self-conscious about "talking to yourself."

If you prefer to practice without background music, then do so. Or you may try music, then practice without music and decide which way is better for you.

Before you begin, be prepared to make the following experiments *not* in an effort to discover your speech *defects*. If you have a malformation, such as a tongue with an extremely short cord on the underside, if you have adenoids, if you have had any injury to your lips or mouth, you need professional analysis and assistance.

You are going to be studying your own personal speech patterns. You will be able to see some, to hear others, and to feel and to understand the balance.

A. Speech patterns you can see

Stand in front of the mirror. *Talk.*

1. THE KIND OF MOUTH AND JAW

a) The wide mouth with a square jaw. Compare the action of this mouth to a bear trap. It hinges strongly and clamps down firmly, but it might trap a flat, lazy tongue behind the teeth. This mouth structure usually has fine teeth, an excellent bite, but speech tends to be trapped and slips back. Say words with "t's" and "th's." Do you see the tip of your tongue? When you come to the exercises, concentrate on the vowels used with D-L-T-TH-ST. NOTE.—In doing the exercise, keep the teeth slightly apart. Don't let that jaw clamp down.

b) The narrow mouth with a jaw lacking strength. This type of mouth often has teeth that are crowded and, sometimes, protrude. In extreme cases, the gums are inclined to show and this makes lip action a problem. However, projection is not usually a problem. Tones come out easily. The jaws hinge flexibly. The roof of the mouth is arched. This can produce musical tones, but it is necessary to watch for nasal tones. The voice naturally throws high. It sometimes results in a twang.

c) The average mouth opens easily. It is neither hindered by a tight jaw nor by a small opening. You can talk, wiggle it in various shapes, and find that it is mobile. If your speech is not clear, your problem is not basically a structural one. It might be lazy speech habits.

B. Speech patterns you hear

1. VOICE QUALITY

Is it low or high? Is it pleasant or unpleasant? Do you say words with the same intonation and pronunciation as the people around you? How does your tone and pronunciation compare to that of the better national news commentators and announcers? With the advent of radio and television, regional dialects in the United States are becoming less pronounced.

When you do speech exercise, play around with the tone. Try the lowest and the highest of your register. Find the tones pleasant to your ear and use them often. Don't be fooled into thinking that the lowest voice is the best. Low voices can be dull, without color tone, and even difficult to understand. A voice that is too high can be shrill, unpleasant, and irritating, but the upper musical tones can be colorful and charming. Hit it both up and down the scale for a well-modulated and varied tone placement.

2. ENUNCIATION

Here is where you will probably hear your imperfections. Even a trained speaker is apt to become sloppy in enunciation. Listen. Is every consonant and vowel given its proper value? Listen and watch. Could you lip-read yourself in the mirror? If you cannot, why not? It could be because you are not forming the words completely. You may be slurring the consonants together. Your vowels might not be clearly enough formed to *float* the word. If you were singing, you would find you cannot sustain a tone on a consonant. They only join together the vowel-notes, so to speak. IMPORTANT.—After this analysis, practice in front of the mirror for improvement of your speech. Concentrate on your "enunciation." However, beware of developing a chop-chop speech, with every consonant sharply spit out.

Attention should be given to the rhythm of speech. Clearness of vowels and consonants must be there, but also, there has to be a tune pattern in order to make it easy for the listener. Little words should not be overemphasized. Let them fall in their proper place. If a sentence is long and involved, avoid plowing through it, slapping equally at each syllable. That will not make it clearer. Instead, divide it up. Fit all the groupings of words into their relative positions. Then, say it. You will find that it will be more simple to say and more easily understood.

For example: *Mr. John McLeod, president of Amertex, the third textile factory to be built in this town, arrived to discuss the dedication of the new school.* Basically, Mr. John McLeod arrived. He arrived to discuss the dedication,—of what? The new school. Who is Mr. McLeod? He is not just "the president" or "the president of Amertex," but "the president of Amertex, the third textile factory to be built in this town." Rhythm-wise, *he arrived to* is the key or base structure. You will notice in breaking up a long sentence, thoughts are presented in proper relation to the main thought. Commas and even periods give away to unseen punctuation or the grouping and rhythm of presenting the ideas. With this thought process applied, you will not be so inclined to emphasize words instead of thoughts. A modifying word should never have overemphasis, unless it is to distinguish it specifically. A modifying word is often in a hyphenated position. "The third factory" —"the new school." It is only "the *third* factory" when the first and second factories are being discussed, and it is necessary to designate the third as a special one in relation to them. The same would be true with the school.

C. Speech patterns—feeling and understanding

In spite of vocal training, diction exercises, and even public speaking classes, there are people who feel they do not speak well and are always striving to find new methods of improvement.

In front of the mirror, talk to yourself as you talk to others. The voice should sound natural. The words are formed correctly. Then, watch yourself. If there is an apparent lack, it may be an inward problem stemming from poor health or a lack of will. If you do not have good health, if you are feeling depressed, if you have a personal problem that causes anxiety, it is difficult to exert yourself to speak vibrantly. If you understand what it is that may be bothering you, it is possible to remedy it. Heart, lung, sinus, asthmatic, or migraine patients tend to speak without causing "vibration." They subconsciously "hush" themselves. Relaxed speech never hurts anyone. If anything, concentration on the simple "exhaling" relaxation would be a benefit. As speech tensions diminish, so will physical tensions, or vice versa.

Then, you may think it is strange to say that some people just do not have the "will" to talk well, but basically, they might not care for people, or possibly they have not enough vital interest in things about them to exert themselves for others. If you wish to speak effectively, no matter how small a "greeting" or how lengthy a profound "speech," *give forth* with a direct, forthright, energetic effort to reach out to those outside *yourself!*

LET US GET TO WORK IN FRONT OF THE MIRROR

A. The vowels. A-E-I-O-U (AY—EE—EYE—OH—YOU)

1. *Whisper them.* Watch closely in the mirror. Can you distinguish one from the other? Can you lip-read them?
2. *Prolong the whisper.* Stand about eighteen inches from the mirror. Put your hands up, palms facing the mirror. NOW
3. *Push the vowels out* until your hands touch the mirror. Just whisper. Work for perfect formation. Each vowel has its own position. JUST WHISPER AND WATCH.
4. *Speak the vowels with minimum voice.* Use the least possible voice but DO NOT reduce any effort in forming the vowels. Use the same care in formation as when you whispered.
5. *Speak the vowels in a normal conversational tone.* Still DO NOT reduce the amount of effort.

6. *Speak the vowels with maximum volume.* Use the hands outward on this again. DO NOT RAISE the voice. Just use it directly forward.

7. *Raise the voice.* Call into the next room with the vowels. Let them prolong and curve upward and out and OVER THERE-er-er-er! THE VOWELS ARE THE FLOATING POWER OF YOUR SPEECH. Watch yourself closely. In steps 1, 2, 3, and 4, there should be absolutely no reduction of effort. In step 5, there is a slight reduction, and in step 6, there is greater exaggeration. Form each vowel carefully. Each one is distinctive. It is just as unattractive to use too much effort as too little. Awareness of proper vowel formation is enormously important.

B. The vowels plus the consonants

Always start an exercise with your lips slightly apart. Feel air in your mouth.

Try the following four steps. Stay in front of the mirror.

1. Whisper "the group."

2. Say "the group" with a strong but medium voice.

3. Call (don't yell) "the group." (The object is to gain range, strength, and ascending tone practice on this one).

4. Drop the voice to normal and say "the group" as rapidly and clearly as possible. Use enough effort to make it EXPLOSIVE.

5. If lack of forcefulness is your problem, use this number 5. Clench your hand into a fist. Simultaneously, with your speaking of "the group," punch out your fist with each combination. Punch hard— use more effort in speaking.

C. Breathing

Proper breathing is necessary for the ease, firmness, steadiness, support, resonance, and control of a *good* voice.

1. Good posture: feet comfortably placed, six inches to one foot apart. Lean forward; lean backward; establish the center of balance.

2. Assume above position. Relax and bend forward from the hips letting arms and hands fall limply down. Very slowly straighten up, beginning this upward movement in the region of the diaphragm. Allow shoulders to slip slowly into position. Don't force them or adjust them voluntarily; don't pull back. Repeat several times until the chest feels at ease.

3. If there is any throat (neck) tension, drop your head and permit it to roll forward and down in complete relaxation. (Left shoulder down to chest; right shoulder down to chest; etc.)

4. Set up natural center of breathing—the epigastrium (region of the diaphragm). This is a natural center of activity, and when you get control of this area, you increase your self-command generally. Place hands at center and side, and inhale (should be extension of this area); then exhale (should be decrease of the area). Inhale, counting 1-2-3-4; hold; exhale, counting 1-2-3-4. Practice breath control early each morning as it will help to start each day with an awareness that you are now working on voice improvement. Do breathing exercises approximately eight times in the beginning, then increase each week. Also, hold count to five; then increase to six; then increase to seven. Avoid excessive exercises at first, as you may become dizzy.

5. Raise arms above head and clasp hands; in this position inhale and exhale. Action will be at the epigastrium.

Try the following experiment in front of your mirror:
Cut a soda straw in short pieces of about three inches. Stick one in your mouth. Exhale by blowing out of it. Hold the breath for a few counts. Now, start pulling the air through the straw slowly. SLOWLY. . . . SLOWLY. . . . fill yourself up with air. Watch yourself in the mirror. DO NOT LET YOUR SHOULDERS RISE. You are not filling your lungs by raising your shoulders. Keep the torso steady. In the last moments, when your lungs are completely filled and pressing strongly against your ribs, there is a slight lift of the whole rib cage. This comes from below. The neck muscles remain unchanged. Do this exercise five times, watching in the mirror. Remove the straw. If there is an ability to relax, most healthy people, without a mechanical obstruction, do breathe well. They breathe well enough to support social speech. Relax after practicing breathing, and you will find your normal breathing has improved. Sometimes lack of breath accompanies lack of thinking. It is imperative to coordinate thinking with your speech for maximum effectiveness.

D. The voice level

Put aside your mirror and sharpen your ears. Take the simple question, "How are you today?" See how many vocal levels you can apply. Try the BOTTOM STEP (speaking in low tones)— THE MIDDLE STEP (average tones)—THE HIGH STEP (tones above your normal range). It is possible that you can control the tone steps in your voice well enough to put that phrase on five tonal levels. Remember that changing the volume of your voice is not altering the tonal level.

Just TALKING LOW is probably not your best voice. A HIGH PITCH can be irritating, although, generally, a high voice has a better possibility of having a "singing musical" quality. Think of a base viol. It has very little vibration. Although a violin might get shrill if not played with skill, it does have great vibration and can be tremendously varied and appealing in tone. Select a level of voice that is best for YOU and that allows for considerable variation between the lower and the upper range.

E. Placement and the tongue

USE the phrase, "I want it at the tip of my tongue." HOLD YOUR NOSE and say it. Do you hear the nasal tones? The vibrations actually jump into your nose. Try to talk without this happening. Start it with "OH." This is a vowel that comes closest to being universally pure. Fewer people, even with regional speech problems or incorrect placements, pervert "O." Use it preceding any sentence to start on an open tone. After the "OH" floats out, make certain the rest of the sentence does not SLIP back. The BEST PLACEMENT you can SEE. In front of your mirror, say, "I want it at the tip of my tongue." Watch and listen! If it is nasal, say, "Oh! I want." Do you hear the "t?" DO NOT say, "I wan-tit." Separate it. "I want it." Then, NOT "ad the"— but "at the." NOT "tippa m' tongue"—but "tip of my tongue." Watch the tongue move during this practice.

Does it delicately "tip" the words out? If not, continue the mirror practice. Place your forefinger a few inches in front of your mouth. Try to reach it with the tip of your tongue. Try hard. Try to POINT it. Reach! With your mouth open, try to draw it back STRAIGHT. Don't curl it. Shoot it out straight again and try to touch that finger. Draw it back slowly— STRAIGHT. Reach out slowly again, STRETCHING and POINT- ING. When beginning this exercise, do it only ten times. If the tongue has been allowed to become lazy, muscle soreness will result. This exercise is fine to do in front of the mirror in the morning. It increases the flow of saliva. If your tongue is under control, effective speech comes more easily.

While practicing, remember SPEECH is an INDIVIDUAL THING. Try to use a pleasant tone, speak with care, but take care not to develop an artificial, stilted manner. If your mirror can teach you how to improve your speech, let it reflect you COMPLETELY and the MOST ATTRACTIVE YOU possible. Raise your head with spirit, open your mouth with confidence, exert yourself to communicate with your fellow man,—SPEAK! Let your personality flow forth uninhibited, and beautifully for- tified by TONE and WORDS.[1]

---

[1] "How to Improve Your Speech" was written in collaboration with Dr. Georgette Mc- Gregor, lecturer on public speaking and effective speech for the University of Cali- fornia, Los Angeles, California. Printed through the courtesy of Dr. McGregor.

EFFECTIVE
MANAGEMENT
COMMUNICATIONS

Our job is to make this vast network of lines and instruments
and switching systems more freely and easily useful to everyone;
so that we can say to each telephone user in each community,
'All this is at your service—and there will be more.'

FREDERICK R. KAPPEL, President,
American Telephone and Telegraph Company

EVERY SUCCESSFUL businessman knows that the old
cliché about the customer always being right is very true indeed,
and not a bit old-fashioned. It is just one of the facts in a highly
competitive free economy, that whenever a business firm fails to
meet its customer's needs and tastes, it loses business.

New methods of using your telephone service can make your
business seem ahead of the rest to customers who call you or
whom you call.

During his lifetime, the average man uses the telephone approximately 8,760 hours. However, a salesman, executive, or
employee in a sales office frequently uses the telephone 8,760
hours within a few years, or within several years.[1]

The livelihood of the man answering the telephone and the
business of his company, in part, are dependent upon his efficient
use of it. Yet in many cases this man learns how to say "hello,"
and to handle the call without giving any constructive thought to
the benefits that might have been derived from efficient handling
of the call.

---

[1] Reprinted through the courtesy of *Rough Notes* from an article, "10 Suggestions to
Help Improve Telephone Efficiency" by Mona Ling.

243

Without intending to do so, this person frequently does great damage to his firm in the loss of prestige and business. The tragedy of this situation is that it takes less time to handle a call efficiently, and the rewards are great in good public relations and increased profits.

Robert Sheehan wrote a report on the unwritten rules of executive deportment in the use of the telephone for *Fortune Magazine*. Some of these ideas are reprinted through the courtesy of *Fortune Magazine*.

THE OBLIGATIONS OF THE OFFICE

Actually, it is the topmost officers who are usually most meticulous about their manners, and most prodigal with their time for the sake of the amenities. Nearly 40 per cent of some 150 company presidents interviewed for this report claimed they answer their own telephones without any screening whatsoever. People who call from the other end of the line might well be astonished at this claim; but, in any event, presidents can give good reasons why the practice *should* be followed. The president of a large midwestern insurance company, who does answer his phone (and also dials his own numbers), says, "I find that 95 per cent of the calls coming in are ones I want to take. Why screen out the 5 per cent of nuisance calls at the risk of irritating the other 95 per cent?" [2]

But it was the president of an aircraft company who put the problem most vividly. "Suppose," he says, "I lose ten or fifteen minutes a day taking fruitless calls. But then Captain Eddie Rickenbacker urgently phones me long-distance from a pay station at hell-and-gone somewhere. Do I want him juggled around from secretary to secretary, or quizzed on who he is and what he wants?" Somehow, the picture of Eddie Rickenbacker sweating it out in a phone booth, his face glowering under those fierce eyebrows, seems to clinch the case for accepting the unscreened call.

---

[2] Reprinted through the courtesy of *Fortune Magazine*.

MOST EXECUTIVES ARE NEVER INACCESSIBLE

The majority of executives, however, still feel the need for screening, if for no other reason than to divert calls that properly should go to other people in the organization. Even so, most such executives insist that they are never inaccessible, or as one president phrased it, "No one who calls and requests to speak to me personally is ever refused." At the very least, they want the screening process to be as subtle and painless as possible. For a secretary to ask, "Who's calling?" or "What did you wish to speak to him about?" is now considered a criminal offense. "May I tell him who's calling?" is just about the limit of allowable inquisitiveness.

Some executives, nevertheless, foolishly hide behind the skirts of their secretaries, a breach of business etiquette on a par with the table ostrich who explores his teeth under cover of his napkin. The genuinely perfect secreatry, of course, is one who never permits a breath of suspicion that *she* is deciding whether or not the caller shall be connected with her boss. A secretary's words can kill. It is amusing to learn, for instance, that the phrase "He's in conference" is now regarded as utterly cornball, and in fact offensive, though the equally elusive "He's in a meeting" is permissible. But the best practice of all, it is agreed, is for the secretary to give the caller a precise idea of what the executive is doing, e.g., "He's holding a budget session with the divisional vice-presidents right now. May he call you when he's free?" Such candor is disarming and preserves the caller's self-esteem. Of course, it's important that the executive *does* call back when he's free, else the fraudulence of the whole routine is exposed, and the sting of the rebuff is compounded.

DON'T MAKE PARTY WAIT ON LINE

But the supreme telephone insult, virtually all executives agree, is to place a call through your secretary, and make the party at the other end of the line hold the connection until you're ready to come on. Says an otherwise uncholeric executive, "When I answer my phone, and a female voice says, 'Please hold on a minute, Mr. Zilch is calling.' I promptly hang up. Let Mr. Zilch call back, and let his be the voice that speaks when I say, 'Hello.' " Peculiarly, this breach is often committed by those who get most indignant when it is done to them.

TELEPHONE CALLS WHILE VISITORS ARE PRESENT

There is one point, however, that the rule books usually do not discuss. Should an executive accept telephone calls while visitors are present? On the one hand, it is embarrassing to a visitor, and an imposition on his time, to be required to sit and gawk while the host-executive takes call after call, some of them obviously confidential in nature. On the other hand, it may be practically essential for the executive to answer some of the calls, or, if the visit is a lengthy one, his secretary may stack up more deferred calls than he is able to handle adequately. Some executives merely offer a brief "Beg pardon," and brazen it out. A better practice is for the executive to anticipate, if possible, such calls as are critical, and, by prearrangement with his secretary, have them put through. At the outset of the interview, he can then say to his visitor, "I am expecting an important call, which, with your permission, etc. . . ." If the call does come, some executives prefer to excuse themselves and take the call in an anteroom. If done gracefully, it is more comforting to the visitor, who doesn't then have to go through a foolish pantomime to prove he's no eavesdropper. If feasible, of course, the best behavior is to quench all calls. But here again, some subtlety is in order. The overt command to "Hold all calls, Miss Betterby" may be flattering to the visitor, but more likely it makes him edgy and apprehensive.

THE MOST COURTEOUS U.S. COMPANIES

In the course of some 150 interviews around the country, executives were asked by *Fortune* to nominate companies of outstanding courtesy. Preponderantly, the selections were provincial in character—neighboring companies, local banks and utilities, and insurance offices. And in almost all cases, the regional telephone company came in for a bow. But of nationally known companies, the following ranked among the top in number of mentions:

Brown-Forman Distillers	Monsanto
Crown Zellerbach	J. P. Morgan & Company
Du Pont	Reynolds Metals
General Electric	Standard Oil of California
General Motors	U.S. Steel

PERSONAL EVALUATION

Robert J. Alander, former advertising director for *Miami News* and the *Charlotte Observer*, said that hundreds of books had been written about selling techniques but not about personal habits. He believes that more books should be written that deal primarily with personal evaluation, as well as with faults of salespeople.

It is true that people do not improve their personality or communication skills or faults until an evaluation is made. You will continue to make the same mistakes until proper evaluation has been made. Only then can you take steps to correct your mistakes.

Many years ago in Atlanta, Robert Alander and four men in the sales business became somewhat critical of each other in a conversation. They agreed to form a "Mutual Admiration Society" to meet once a month for the sole purpose of frankly discussing whatever it was, or whatever they did, that the others didn't like. They agreed to be completely honest, saying nothing nice about each other. Frankly, the first meeting was a stunner. Robert Alander knew automatically that he was just about perfect, and knew he was quite familiar with any faults he might have, or so he thought.

"What the other four told me," says Robert, "that they disliked about me as a person has had a bigger effect on my life (that was twenty-one years ago) than any one thing I have experienced or any books I've read. It was an eye opener, believe me! I had no trouble criticizing the other people in the group, and I felt rather sorry for them when I let them have it. They were selfish in their relationship with other people, conceited, etc.

"I was mighty shocked when they got around to telling me about my faults. It was just too impossible to believe, and yet, now when I look back, all of them were justified. They were completely right in their criticism, and now, after these twenty-one years have passed, I still find it a daily need to correct these shortcomings and keep in mind that knowing them is not correcting them. They will remain problems of mine the rest of my life.

"I think we need more 'Mutual Admiration Societies.' I think, too, many of us go through life unaware of our own personality shortcomings. Let's know ourselves better. Let's realize the need of a personal evaluation and then do something about it." [3]

NO TIME FOR SLOW ANSWERS

A company's telephone service and its product are linked so closely together in most businesses that it is vital for your telephone service to be as up-to-date as the product you sell or the service you render.

Dialing long-distance direct, for example, or having extension users "on the line" when called parties answer, are policies that many businesses follow, with the customer's viewpoint in mind.

And then, the attitude of your switchboard attendants and extension users toward the people who call your company—in the human relations sense—can greatly affect your business. Today's customer demands to be treated with respect. He wants to be recognized as an individual, with special wants and needs that you can meet. If you can transmit to him the fact that you recognize his individual importance, then you're in business to stay.

---

[3] Reprinted through the courtesy of *The Retail Advertising and Sales Promotion Manual* of the National Research Bureau.

Mrs. Jean Brown, a PBX instructor for Southern Bell in Melbourne, Florida, says, "There is no time for slow answers in the space age."

Mrs. Brown works in the midst of the space-blazing atmosphere of Cape Canaveral, where there is an attention to detail, to timing, to precision, and a dedication to duty that could very well be a guide for all telephone users, no matter what job they do.

Just as the Control Center is responsible for much of the space program's success, your own switchboard is responsible for maintaining smooth business relations with your company's callers. And you may be sure of one thing: there are no slow answers at Canaveral Control.

Mrs. Brown says, "I like to compare Canaveral's Central Control Center, which keeps in touch with the astronauts in outer space, to a PBX switchboard that serves as the 'Go' key to communications for your business.

"Considering slow answers as one of the major problems of any PBX operation, I would recommend a personal countdown on your operating methods to see what can be done to answer customers more promptly and to improve the over-all speed with which you handle calls.

"A-OK" answers require a certain rhythm, a smooth and cool-headed attitude toward handling each call promptly. The efficient PBX attendant does not let signals pile up. One important way you can avoid this is by learning overlap operations. This will enable you to give courteous and well-timed attention to each caller.

"To accomplish an efficient PBX operation and to eliminate slow answers require planning and organization. Consider these points:

1. There should be understanding and agreement about the need for good telephone usage among all the people in your business organization. Extension users need to use good telephone techniques. If more than one operator works at a PBX board, each must learn to combine her operating skills with those of her teammates.
2. Your PBX board should be maintained in a neat and orderly manner.

Records should be arranged so they will help you work without fuss and bother. Tickets and other materials should not clutter up your board.

3. Learning efficiency (and working closely with your telephone PBX instructor in this) is important. Slow answers can be caused by inattention, but generally they are the result of improper training. It takes skill in overlapping as well as sure motions in establishing connections to solve the problem of slow answers.

"Fine equipment like a Bell System PBX board works well only when it is properly operated. As astronaut John Glenn said, 'There's still room for man in this machine age.' And certainly there's plenty of room for the alert, courteous PBX attendant who does not fly into outer space but keeps her feet firmly on the ground when it comes to the question of answering customers promptly and giving good PBX service."

TELEPHONE SAVES LOSSES

The concept of the telephone in business is constantly changing, because modern businesses have learned what the telephone contact can do if telephone service is planned from the customer's point of view.

In the April 1962 issue of *The American Salesman*, this brief item appeared.[4] To cut down on retailers' one-billion-dollar-a-year losses from bad checks, Telecredit, Inc., of Los Angeles, offers telephone verification. Telecredit has consumers' credit records, filed by driving license number, on IBM computer. In a few seconds after information on would-be check-casher is fed into machine, rating flashes on.

TELEPHONE ANSWERING SERVICES HANDLE CALLS

Telephone answering services (TAS) are literally taking the "no" out of "no answer" by acting as telephone secretaries for

---

[4] Reprinted through the courtesy of *The American Salesman*, 51 East 42nd Street, New York 17, New York.

business and professional people on the move who find it expedient
to have their telephones answered at all hours. For a monthly fee,
the answering services handle important calls that might other
wise go unanswered.

The industry is now almost fifty years old. It began primarily
as a service for physicians but expanded to include telephone
ordering, monitoring of fire and burglar alarm systems, civil
defense, stalled elevator service, wake-up services, and many more.
Telephone secretaries also make travel and lodging reservations
and appointments, dispatch repairmen, and perform a variety of
related secretarial duties.

In the operation of a telephone answering service, secretaries
must be hired and scheduled with the goal of providing courteous,
fast, efficient service. The telephone companies work closely with
the answering services to help them keep abreast of the latest
equipment and techniques in service.

The guides for efficient PBX operators also apply to the telephone secretary:

1. Pleasing voice and friendly manner
2. Prompt answers and disconnects
3. 30-second progress reports
4. Attention to overlaps
5. Scanning for signals
6. Individual poise
7. Pleasant personality

To improve the quality of service, TAS owners are giving more
attention to work studies that measure calls in relation to work
time, thus pinpointing service problems, such as switchboard
overload. In many cases, they have found, as a result of study,
that more client lines can become available through uniform
distribution of lines using equipment already in place.

A recent Bell System study also found that the telephone secretary equipped with a prescribed list of answering phrases does
a better over-all service job than the secretary who does not. Use
of prescribed phrases, instead of an "ad-lib" approach helps the

secretary to stay in control of the conversation and to give faster service.

It is estimated that the nation's 2,500 answering service bureaus, which employ 42,000 people, handle a billion calls annually and serve approximately 10 per cent of all telephone business customers.

Mrs. Aline King, owner of a large answering service in Shreveport, Louisiana, has watched her business grow from five customers in 1949 to a thousand today. This is symbolic of the mushroom growth of TAS since World War II.

Mrs. King sees an unlimited future for the telephone answering industry. "People can't afford to be away from their telephones today," she says. "We are filling that need and are helping them to be more flexible in their business." Mrs. King's predictions for the future: even more personalized service and an expansion into the residence market. Night or day, the telephone secretaries try to have the right answer. Their watchword is service—good service.

As my work takes me throughout the United States and Canada, I have had to rely upon the services of telephone answering services. At times, I maintain a service in Los Angeles, Miami, and Detroit and work between these three headquarters. My permanent business service is the Telephone Answering Service, Inc., 3049 East Grand Boulevard, Detroit 2, Michigan. These operators can locate me within a few hours, sometimes within minutes, wherever I am working or traveling. Obviously, during large Sales Workshops or Training Programs, I cannot be reached by telephone, which is not the fault of the operators but is the nature of my business. These operators are very efficient and I could not conduct my business without the capable services of telephone answering services.

1,000 WORDS A MINUTE

Dataspeed, a new development in teletypewriter service, is based on the principle of tape transmission and is capable of transmitting or receiving more than one thousand words a minute—ten times faster than the latest TWX machine. The high-speed system utilizes Data-Phone to transmit information over the regular telephone network.

Figuratively speaking, Sue Jones is doing her work ten times faster these days in the communications center of the National Presto Manufacturing Company at Jackson, Mississippi.

As a TWX attendant, Sue was responsible for transmitting a heavy volume of information between Jackson and the company's home office in Eau Claire, Wisconsin—items such as shipping orders, payrolls, and general correspondence. While this responsibility still belongs to Sue, Dataspeed has made the tenfold difference.

The new service uses a standard five-level punched paper tape that can be produced by any teletypewriter with a tape punch attachment. Dataspeed transmitting and receiving units are housed in separate cabinets that contain the tape unwinders and rewinders. Controls are mounted on front shelves and the Data-Phone set is built into the cabinet. A tape reader attached to the TWX machine converts the received tape to page copy.

National Presto, which manufactures home appliances, has found the new service well-tailored to handle its flow of volume information. Transition from conventional TWX posed no particular problem for Sue Jones. Within a week, she became fully adept at operating the system and was sending in five minutes data that once took an hour.

FIRST INSTALLATION OF BELL SYSTEM'S NEW DATA-PHONE

The first installation in the United States of an assembly line production model of the Bell System's new Data-Phone equipment has been made at the Coral Gables Federal Savings and Loan Assocaition.

Bill D'Amico, district sales manager at Coral Gables Southern Bell Company, said the few previous installations in the country were made with experimental models. These first production line sets have provided the missing link in Coral Gables Federal's new automated accounting system, enabling one business machine to talk to another over telephone lines.

With the conversion to automated accounting, the four branch offices in Dade County previously accumulated all transactions on eight-channel punched tape. These tapes were then sent by messenger service to headquarters at the end of each day for conversion to cards for insertion into computers to extend balances and add interest.

The problem was to get the tapes to the headquarters throughout each day, so that balances for each branch office could be computed and made ready for the next day's business.

Southern Bell representatives, working with Harry Ennis, assistant vice-president, pointed out how Data-Phone service could solve these problems. Ennis called in a business machine salesman to work with their representatives. Data-Phone service has enabled Coral Gables Federal to streamline its entire operation through fast, accurate transmission of tapes. In addition, the high cost of overtime clerical help to arrive at these balances has been eliminated.

DATA-PHONE TRANSMISSION SYSTEMS

Alexander Graham Bell would have been awe-struck, had he been present to witness the latest development of his invention, which was unveiled by Soroban Engineering, Inc. at its Port Malabar, Florida, facility on April 19.

At a special showing for the press and industry representatives, Soroban displayed its Data-Phone transmission system, which provides for the high-speed transmission of bulk information at extremely low cost.

These systems utilize the Bell Telephone Company's new and improved model 201 Data-Phone Subset, and utilize these subsets to their optimum.

It is possible and practical through the use of Soroban's equipment to transmit and receive information at the rate of 300 codes per second, or 2,850 written words per minute. This information can be fed directly to a computer or data-processing system as received.

Economical? The answer is an emphatic "Yes." Eight thousand, five hundred and fifty words can be transmitted from Cape Canaveral, Florida, to Washington, D.C., for $1.15. The same amount of information can be transmitted from Cape Canaveral to San Francisco for $1.75 or to New York City for $1.20. It is possible with the use of Soroban's high-speed Data-Phone transmission system to transmit the complete text of the book, *Gone with the Wind*, from Cape Canaveral to New York City for a total transmission cost of $72.00. This figure is based on a transmission of 513,000 words.

Soroban, headed by Charles F. West, president, produces quality systems and equipment for use in the fields of data processing, office automation, numerical control, high-speed communications, data logging, and ground test support.

In this day and age, businessmen have to be concerned with effective telephone communication at all levels. An individual must learn to talk to another individual effectively. An executive must learn to talk to his associates across the country and transmit important information to them efficiently and rapidly. Today, machines talk to machines and conduct as much business within a few minutes as people once conducted within several hours or several days.

WISE INVESTMENT OF TIME

The businessman today knows that inter-business selling, as well as direct consumer sales, is dependent on the telephone. Adequate equipment is necessary for good public relations. If equipment is inadequate to keep your telephone doors open, customers soon begin calling someone else. Adequate equipment is necessary for field forces and for widely scattered offices. The businessman today knows that the daily investment of time is important to the operation of the business.

Dr. Paul P. Parker, who has served as personnel consultant to some of the nation's leading corporations, such as General Motors, Ford Motor Company, General Mills, Goodyear Rubber, and Eastman Kodak Company, says, "At birth you inherited half a million—not dollars, but hours. You alone have absolute control over the investment of this half a million. You wouldn't think of throwing five-dollar bills in the gutter and watching them wash away, but how about the indifferent, careless waste of 25 per cent and sometimes 50 per cent, of our time just because we have never learned how to invest it." [5]

In my experience in the training of salesmen and management, I have discovered that a great deal of this wasted time stems from inefficient communication skills and systems. A salesman out in the field will frequently have to write to the home office or regional office for vital information, because long-distance telephone calls are discouraged. While Bill is waiting for a reply to his letter, his competitor gets the business.

Management changes rules, procedures, or policies that they believe will enable the sales forces to operate more efficiently. By the time this information has been transmitted to the sales forces, and questions have been mailed back to the office, and answers have gone back to the sales forces, there is confusion; errors, mistakes, doubts, uncertainties remain with the sales forces for several months. These errors and mistakes must have some influence over sales and profits for a long period of time.

A FAST, FLEXIBLE APPROACH TO VOLUME LONG-DISTANCE SERVICE

In recent months extension users and PBX attendants have discovered a new approach to volume long-distance calling. This

---

[5] Reprinted through permission of Success Motivation Institute, Inc., from the recording *"How to Use Tact and Skill in Handling People."*

is called Wide Area Telephone Service (WATS). This stream-lined optional service offers the customer long-distance calling at a flat monthly charge and makes maximum use of the Bell System's flexible network of telephone circuits and switching systems.

It is designed primarily for the business customer who makes many calls to widely-scattered and distant points and is a supplement for regular long-distance and private-line service.

Here's how the system works:

Using WATS is similar to making a call by Direct Distance Dialing. After a WATS line has been secured, the extension caller or attendant simply dials Access Code one (1), the area code, and telephone number of the called station. Cost to the customer is then determined by the width of the calling area, the number of access lines desired, and whether or not the service is needed full or part-time.

In determining the reach of his interstate Wide Area Service, a caller can choose from six different areas—the sixth, or widest, allowing him to call points outside his home state anywhere within the United States, except Alaska and Hawaii.

Intrastate calling is also available, as a separate service, for the businessman who wishes to include calling within his home state.

Other than in the largest and most populous states, the calling areas follow state boundaries. Areas are established according to a percentage of the total square miles and total telephones of the United States, excluding the customer's home state.

The first area includes all states contiguous to the customer's home state, and, if necessary, other neighboring states, to reach about 10 per cent of the total square miles and telephones in the U.S.

The second area would include the next closest states to reach around 20 per cent of total square miles and telephones; the third area, 40 per cent; the fourth area, 60 per cent; the fifth area, 80 per cent; the sixth area encompasses the entire country, except the home state.

MEASURED TIME SERVICE

If the customer does not wish to use the service full time, he can get "measured time" service at less than the "full time" rate. In "measured time," his basic rate covers use of the service for fifteen hours a month. If he exceeds this usage time, he pays a fixed charge for each additional hour.

Wide Area Telephone Service offers certain advantages to business customers. It is more flexible than private-line service and can be less expensive than comparable use of the regular nationwide message network.

Here are its advantages to customers:

1. Allows calls to most telephones within specified areas, instead of to just certain telephones as in private-line service.
2. Makes circuits of entire general toll switching network available to customers.
3. Provides lower cost long-distance calling for volume use.

With these many advantages, WATS is a big step in the direction of better, more economical long-distance communication. The fact that other steps will have to follow is evidenced by the fact that today's world telephone count of 135 million is expected to grow to half a billion in the next twenty years. Overseas calling is expected to rise from 4 million calls a year to around 100 million.

This vast growth will necessitate an even more flexible nationwide network and new developments, such as electronic switching and "wave guide" transmission systems, will help make it so. Keeping pace with these technological advances, will be other new services to provide more convenient, efficient telephone communications for tomorrow's customers.

COMMUNICATIONS IN THE FUTURE

As astronaut John Glenn orbited the earth, I thought of the tremendous effect space flight would have on communications in the future. Future generations will look back to the beginning of the Space Age and think that life was mighty slow and unexciting. They will wonder how we managed to get along with our backward communication systems. As the future unfolds, it is obvious that life in the end of this century and the beginning of the year 2000 will hold many impressive innovations, particularly in the area of communications and the way it can affect all human endeavor.

But how will future communications affect you and your business? What is in store for you and your telephone system?

Of course, keeping in mind that all predictions are based on certain knowns but are subject to the vagaries of many unknowns, the outlook is overwhelming. We know, for instance, that there are going to be more people demanding the goods and service of your business and ours. Population experts predict that by 1970 there will be about 215 million Americans and by the year 2000, the population will have grown to well over 300 million. More than 75 per cent of these people will be concentrated in our growing metropolitan centers. Annual income will be up. The number of households will expand.

The population explosion, as it is so often called, means that all business—including yours and the telephone industry—will need to find better and more economical ways to serve our customers.

Today, on the drawing boards, in experimental laboratories, and in actual production, are many Bell System developments that will make your communications future bright and help you develop your business operations in the most efficient way.

Within the next few decades, and in some instances sooner, you will see many changes like these!

Could it increase your volume of business if the customer could call in and see the product you sell by Picturephone? Or, how much time would it save you, if sales meetings (even cross-country sales meetings) could be conducted on a face-to-face basis with this telephone innovation? Sounds like a time-saver. Picturephone is definitely a coming development.

By dialing a number at your home, you will be able to turn on the office air-conditioner or heater, or start the operation of various business machines. From the office, you could read meters (such as electricity, gas, or water meters)—all by telephone. Such remote control will be a reality.

You don't have to dial the number on a frequently-called telephone number. Repertory dialers of various sorts are on the market that automatically dial any one of its prerecorded numbers, simply by the press of a button.

Many new telephone instruments are being developed that give the extension users in your business the best service. Touch-tone dialing—on a set in which pushbuttons replace the familiar dial —in a de luxe service is now being tested in several market areas. An "executive ring-back" arrangement is being developed for business use. If an executive calls one of the people in your firm and the called line is busy, a tone will indicate to the called party that his supervisor is attempting to reach him.

PBX JOB WILL BE MUCH EASIER

New PBX boards are being designed with many innovations that will make tne PBX job easier at your office. There will be a wide choice of attractive PBX consoles that will speed operation and improve service. Packaged in a new way, PBX equipment will be easy and economical to install and to move.

Under development is an electronic PBX that consists of a central office "group control" and will give you many advantages in handling your calls.

Many of the new advances are tied in with electronic switching that is now being tested. Because of its "memory" and speed, electronic switching systems will expand telephone possibilities immensely.

Data transmission methods will be so helpful to your business that it is predicted that by 1975, business data carried over Bell System facilities could easily exceed the volume of speech now carried.

Commercial satellite communications will help meet the need for an increase in transoceanic communication. A series of satellites, strategically placed—perhaps eight thousand miles high in the sky, will be able to beam telephone calls and television programs from continent to continent.

YEAR 2000

By the year 2000, everyone might possibly have a telephone with him wherever he goes—something like Dick Tracy's wrist watch radio. This means you'll be able to call almost anyone anywhere in the world or in outer space. Each person might be assigned a telephone number at birth. As long as he lived, the person could be reached at his personal number.

Magazines, newspapers, and other media might be delivered to your business or home instantly by telephone lines.

World-wide flat-rate calling might be possible. Already, the distinction between local and long-distance charges is gradually disappearing.

Banking could be done by telephone. You might walk into a store, write a check for your purchase, and the amount would be immediately posted on your bank records. Meanwhile, the transaction could set an inventory restocking process in motion.

You might visit an art gallery over the telephone screen or be able to call the library and consult reference materials without leaving home.

And to place a call, you might simply speak the numbers into your telephone receiver. The Bell Laboratories has developed an automatic Digit Recognizer that already approaches this idea.

Obviously, as far as the telephone business is concerned, communications in the year 2000 will loom larger in the daily life of everyone, and people will be more dependent on reliable communications facilities than ever before.

Machine—computer machines and electronic brains—will play a major role in our future society. Machines will make for greater ease in living and will allow more leisure for everyone.

For your business, the opportunities in this kind of world can be almost staggering. Your markets will be bigger. You will have new and improved products.

People prefer to do business with a person who thinks clearly and who can state his ideas clearly. People prefer to do business with a company or firm that has a modern communications system.

Our brains, like our telephones, do not come with a set of directions attached. Straight thinking will help us to make our future successful. Proper telephone techniques will help us to step up our ability to communicate effectively with others.

Because of man's desire to awaken a response in another person and to get a reaction, he created a verbal universe. When man built up complex environments, societies, nations, and created a complex verbal universe, he required faster communications.

Whatever the future holds for individuals, communication systems will always be ready to take care of their changing needs. The progress of the peoples of the world is linked with the vast communication facilities. The telephone is vital in communications on land, or sea, or into outer space, as well as inside the home or office.